# THE BOOK OF KELLS

WITH
A STUDY OF
THE MANUSCRIPT
BY
FRANÇOISE
HENRY

*126 colour plates*
*75 monochrome illustrations*

ALFRED A. KNOPF · NEW YORK

1974

# THE BOOK OF KELLS

REPRODUCTIONS
FROM THE MANUSCRIPT
IN TRINITY COLLEGE
DUBLIN

THIS IS A BORZOI BOOK
PUBLISHED BY ALFRED A. KNOPF, INC.
© THAMES AND HUDSON 1974 LONDON

Photography by John Kennedy of 'The Green Studio',
Dublin
Printed and bound by Conzett and Huber, Zurich

ISBN: 0-394-49475-X
Library of Congress Catalog Card Number: 74-7732

*First American Edition*

# CONTENTS

THE AIM OF THIS EDITION is to show the illustration and decoration of the Book of Kells in colour. It includes all the full page illustrations in the manuscript and a representative selection of the ornamentation that is to be found on the text pages. In all 93 pages and 6 half pages are reproduced complete. In every case a recto of the original manuscript has been kept as a right-hand page and a verso as a left-hand page. In addition to these reproductions there are 30 plates of greatly enlarged details from the illustrations.

The photography was carried out by John Kennedy, of The Green Studio, Dublin, in the Library of Trinity College. The page size is based on the size of the largest page of the manuscript. Nevertheless, the image in the whole-page reproductions is not of absolute facsimile size, and this is for technical reasons connected with the photography. Because of the importance of the manuscript the photography had to be carried out under very rigorous conditions. The variation is slight in most cases but in a few reaches a maximum of three per cent.

The pages are identified on the leaves facing the first page of each section – the Preliminaries, the four Gospels separately, and the enlarged details.

# PRELIMINARIES

# *Preliminaries*

The Preliminaries occupy folios 1R–26V. They consist of canon-tables, *Breves causae* (summaries of the Gospels), *Argumenta* (traditional prefaces) and lists of Hebrew names. This section of the Book is incomplete, and it begins in the middle of the list of Hebrew names.

Sadoc

iusupretatus

Sidon

dariuo

Thomas

abysus

Zorobabel

ipsemagist

babilonis

Nabulon

habitaculum

Zaccheus

iustificatussi

ue iustifricandus

*f 2R*

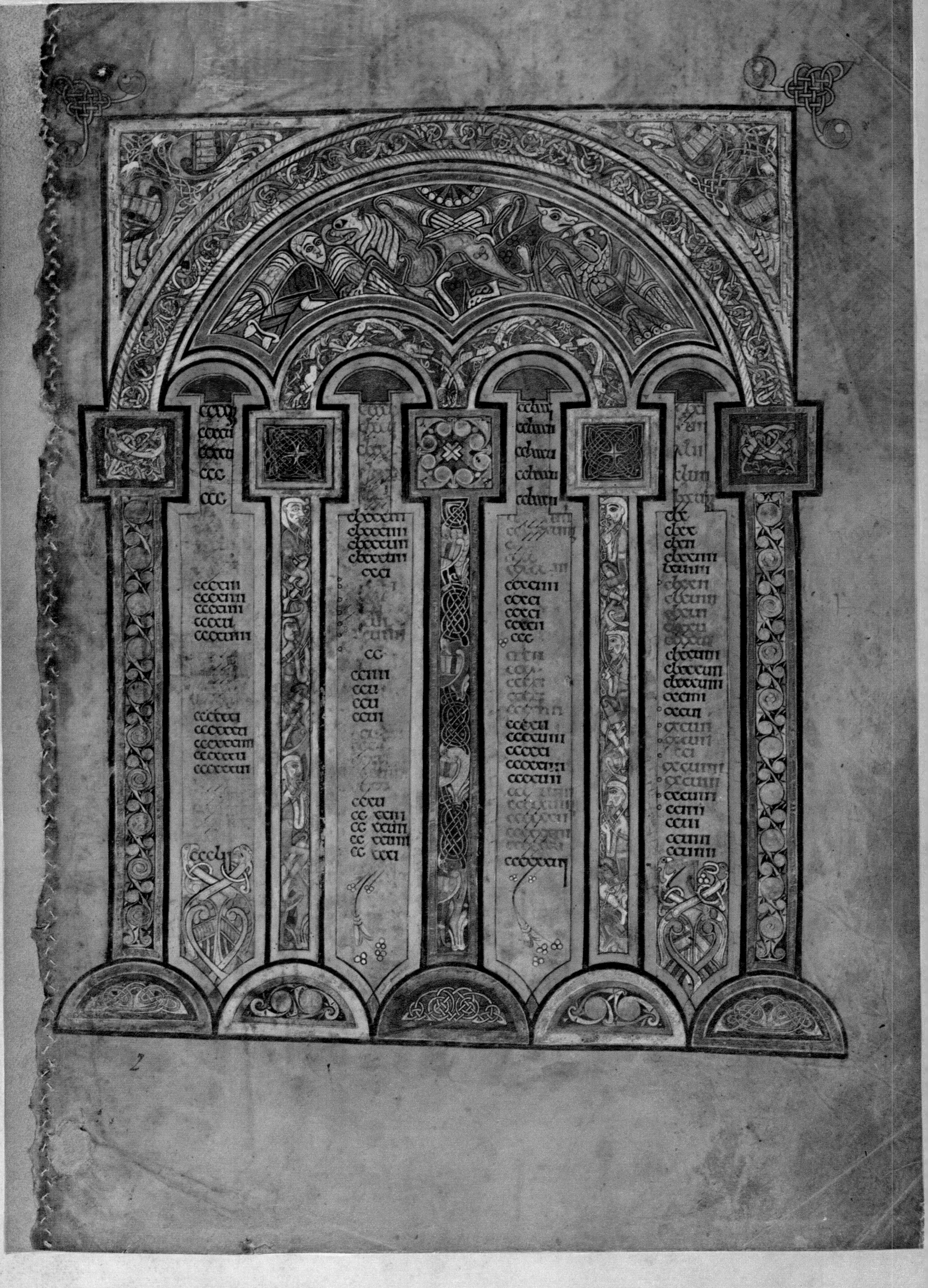

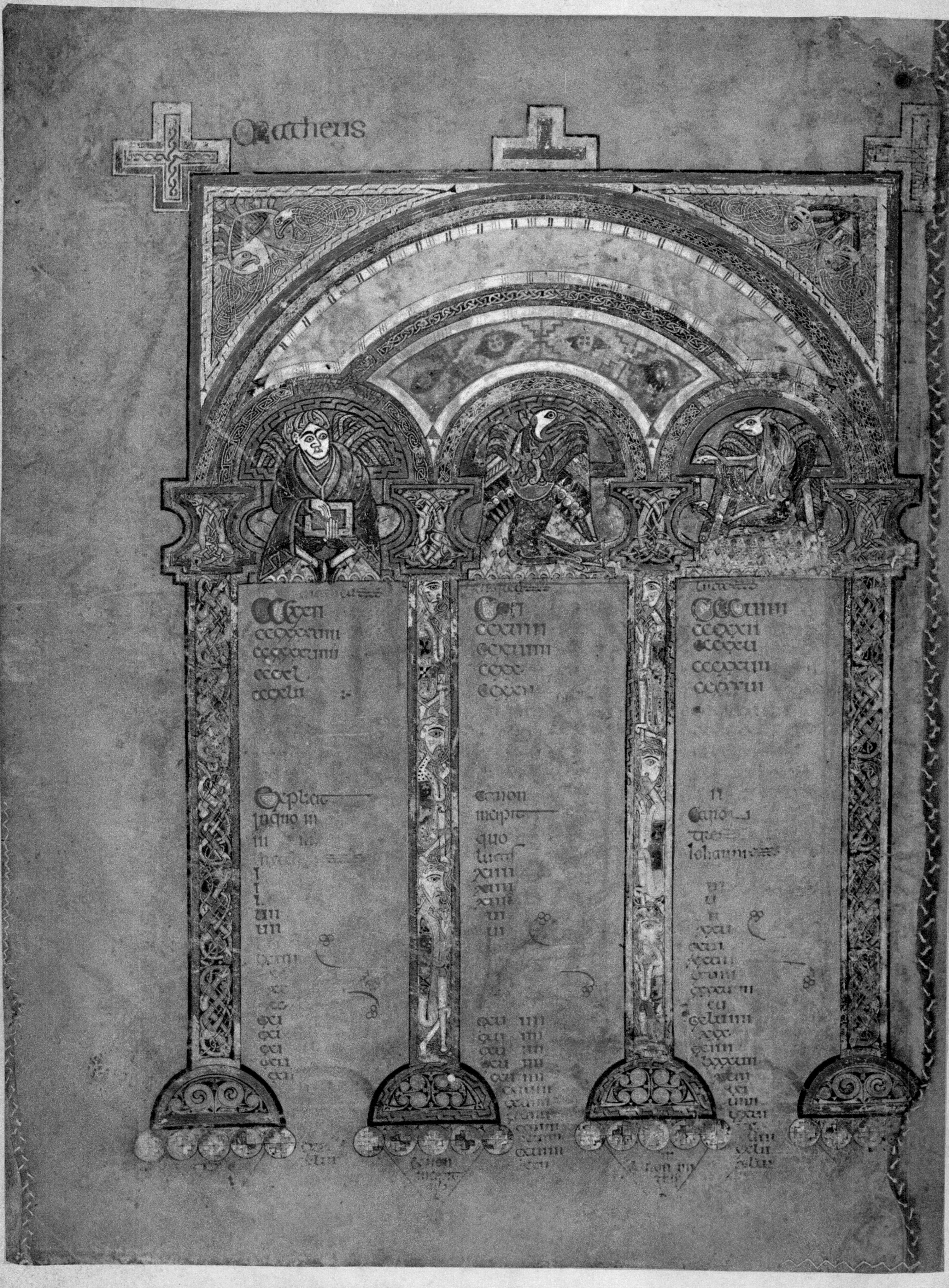
Mattheus

Nativitas xpi in bethleem Iudee angeli minera obtulerunt
et infantes interfecti sunt

Matheus

Quæssicutprimus poni
tur inordine : :

Ituangelium iniudia primus scripsit cuis
uocatio addnin expuplicanis acabus fuit
duorum ingeneratione xpi principia prate

Hannis habo ꝫ uchin le ui

hic supereum spsdi & panns in deserto
temptatus · Et postquam tradatus est ioha
nis prædicans · ihs euocauit discipulos Et

f15v

f16v

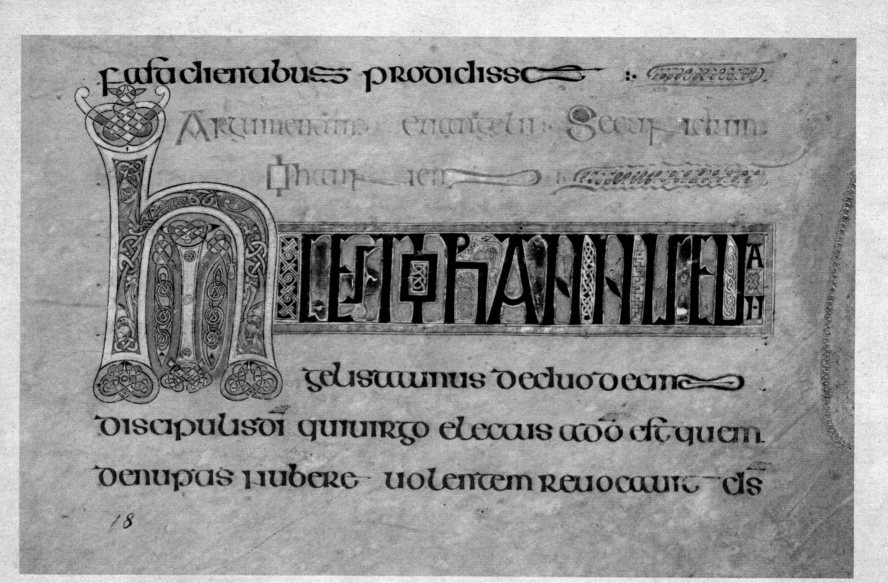

fafacherubus prodidisse :. 

Argumentum euangelii Secundum

Johannem

h iertohannued a
xx
h

gelistuunus deduo ean

discipulisdi quiuirgo electus add estquem

denupas hubere uolentem reuocauit ds

18

riae sacerdoti appa

ruit angelus Etadnuntiauit ei filium iohaz

nen Etidem mariae adnuntiauit angelus

filium ihm :. toribus :. Et uca

Natuitatem ihu adnuntiat angelus pas

14

ecit ·········· porco

Filiam principis resuscitat ihs & mulierem
a profluuio sanguinis saluat

Potestatem dedit ihs discipulis suis demonia
expellere & languores saluare :·

De quinque panib; & duobus piscib; inquinquae
uirorum :· & dicat qui uult tol

Interrogat ihs discipulos quem eum dixerint
lat crucem suam & sequatur me ·

In monte loquebatur cum moyse & helia dis
cendens ihs de monte puerum a demonio
curauit & docebat humilitatem sicut pu
eros fieri electorum prohibito qui non se
quebatur

Dixerunt iacob & iohannis dne uis dica
mus ignem ut psteat helias de caelo :·

Erat quidam uolens sequi te & alio dicit
sequere me & sineme mortuos sepelire mor
tuos suos & ualefac

Inaccena faciatis incor. inclato ut uiuellras. illii

Genasit dns discipulos & pararunt pascha.

dixit sacramentum corporis & sanguinis

sui qumult innobis esse maior erit ministr

Quihaba tollat & peram & quinonhaba

uendat tunicam & emat gladium

Cumuenitionte solus oratsse dixit discipu

lis orate nenurtur intainptationem

Et dixit ihs meiue osculo filium hominis tradis

Et dixerunt adilluni principes sacerdotum si

t ares xps dic nobis & obaudierunt eum

pilato abfirodr

In passione dixit ihs pater dimitte illis

qrinesciunt & cum clatronibus dicit

l dicho mecum eris inparadiso

Post resurrixtionem apparuit ihs duob:

enntab: adillum & apostolis & benedicens

Capascndo mdeli

Iohannis testimonium perhibet eiecto christo
non sum dignus corrigiam calciamenti
eius soluere. Ecce Iohannis christicola
agnus christi qui tollit peccatum mundi.

Ostendit ihs discipulis suis ubi manere. Et
secuti sunt eum. Ubi ihs de aqua uinum fecit
in chana galilaeae. Eiecit ihs de templo omnes uendentes et dixit domus orationis est
domus patris mei. Si quis non renatus fuerit de nouo
et aqua et spu sco non intrabit in regnum ch.
Ubi baptizat ihs et dixit Iohannis discipulis
ego non sum xps. Ubi secessit ihs in iudeam et
ibant in samariam. præ dible eth

Sedens super puteum mulierem samaritanam
et discipulis suis alii laborauerunt et uos in la-
borem ipsorum introistis. Omnis propheta sine
honore est in patria est sua ubi filium reguli sanauit.

Ego rogabo patrem meum . Et mittet uo
bis spm ueritatis ⁝ me diligitis qui
Ego sum uitis uera & pater meus agricola si
cleritis qui maiai do ad patrem
uenis . horantquiuos occiderit putat
se . obsequium do facere . & ritiuaq
habebitis secldaum uidebo uos &
gaudebit cor uestrum & claritas
oculis ihs dixit pater clarifica filium tuum
Pater sce seruaeos Innomine tuo sci est
discipulos & adplacuiu
& duxerunt ihm adclaiaiam & aiaiaui
& deduce dixit ihs discipulo quem di
ligebat . ecce mater tua
Post resurrectionem apparuit ihs disci
pulis & noncredebat thomas & duraim ap
paruit ei increbat eum . thus absce ouib
& audiuo maiufhaara se ihs discipulis erat p quo chains
meus egeguibre me ⁝

# MATTHEW

# Matthew

The Gospel according to St Matthew occupies folios 27V–129V.

19

genuit acham
achas h genuit
ezechiam eze
chias autem
genuit manas
sen manasses
h genuit am
os amos autem
genuit iosiam
iosias h genuit
iechoniam &
fratres eius
in transmigra

tionem babylo
nis. & post tra
lis migratione
babilonis. Ie
chonias genuit
salathiel sala
thiel h genui
sorobabel. so
robabel autem
genuit abiud
abiud autem
genuit eliachi
eliachim

genuit azor  iacob autem

azor autem  genuit ioseph

genuit sadoc  uirum marie

sadoc autem  dequanatus

genuit achim  est ihs quiuoca

achim autem  tur xps

genuit eliud  Omnesergo

eliud autem  generationes

genuit eleaza  ababracham

eleazar autem  usque addauid

genuit mathan  generationes

mathan autem  xiiii Dabd

genuit iacob  uid usque co

31

3R

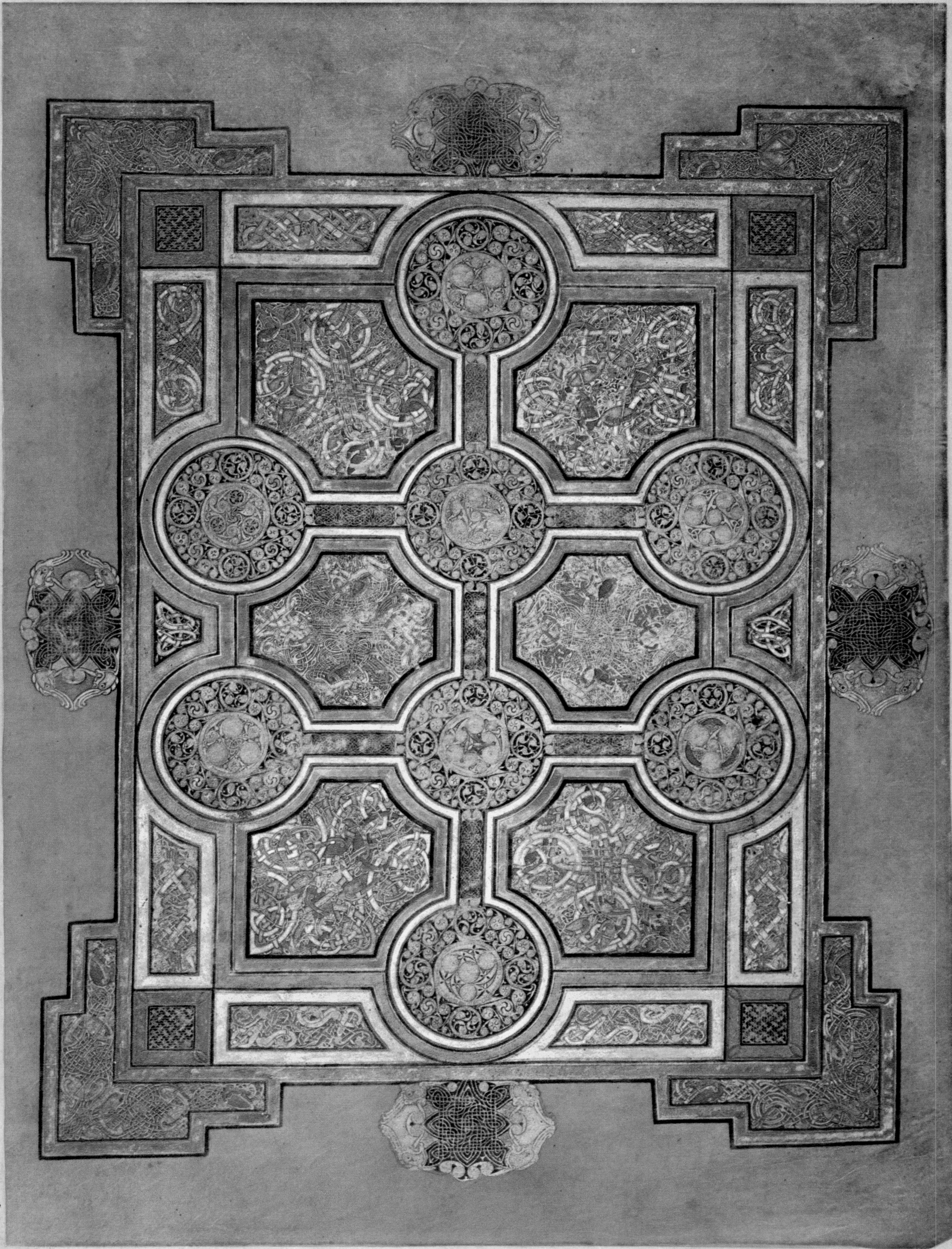

4R

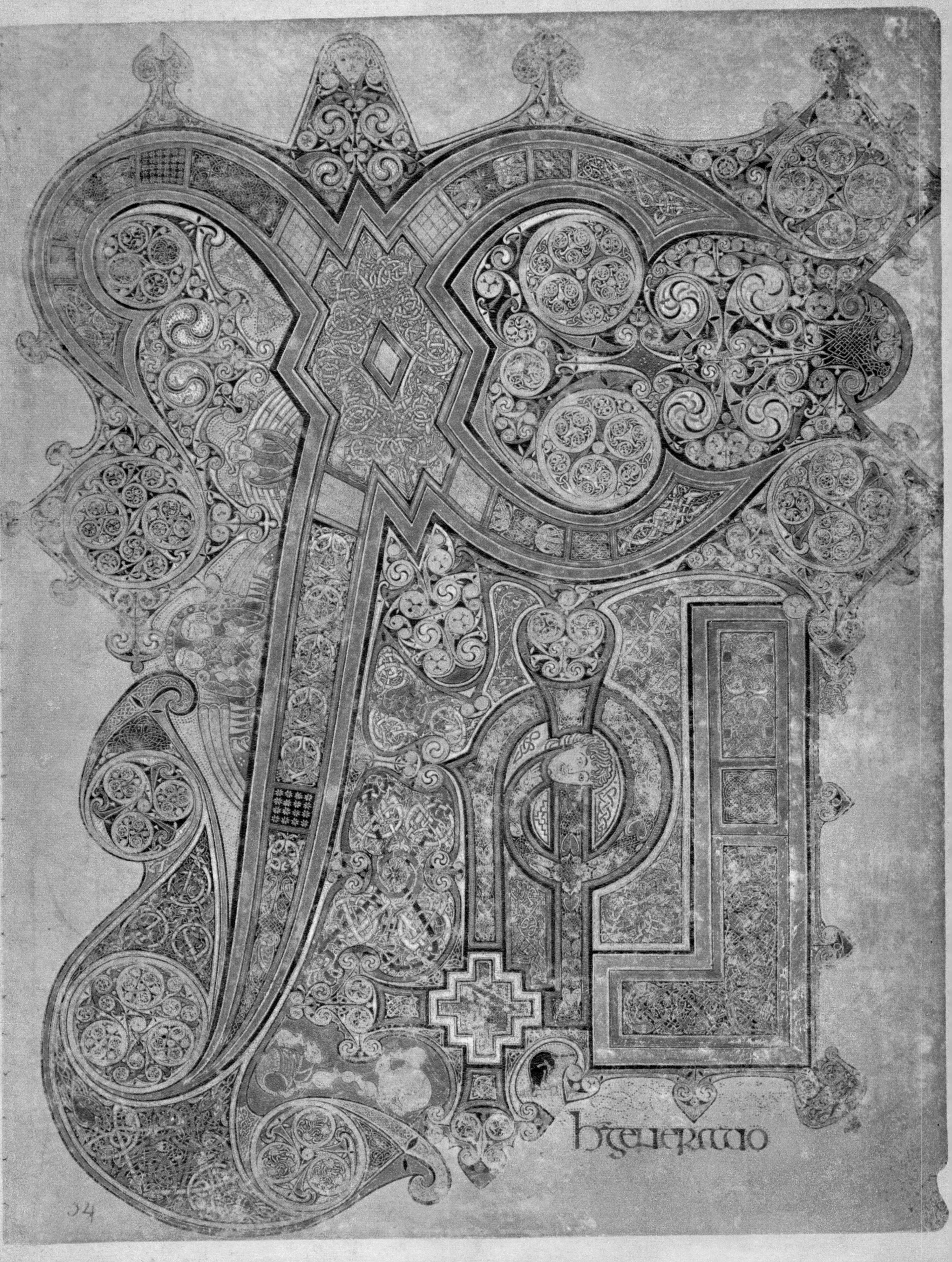

eata pauperes spu quoniam

ipsorum est regnum caelorum·

eata mites quoniam ipsi possi

debunt terram

eata qui lugent nunc quoniam

ipsi consulabuntur

eata quiessuriunt & sitiunt

iustiam quoniam ipsi satu

rabuntur

eata misericordes quoniam

ipsi missericordiam consequnt

eata mundo corde· quoniam

ipsi dm uidebut

eata pacifici quoniam filidi

uocabuntur

eata qui persecutionem pata

untur propter iustiam quon

altair abhominibus

Amen dico uobis receperunt

mercedem suam tu autem cum orabis

intra incubiculum tuum & cluso ostio

tuo orapatrem tuum inabsconso

& pater tuus quiuidet inabsconso red

det tibi

Orantes autem nolite multum lo

qui sicut ethnici putant enim quia

inmulta loquio suo exaudiantur. Nol

te ergo cosimilari eris. Scit enim pa

ter uester quid uobis opus sit ante

quam petatis abeo sic ergo uos orabitis

ur. Homen tuum:

Pater noster qui es incaelis scificetur

adueniat regnum tuum fiat uo

luntas tua sicut incaelo & interra

sicut israhel. farisei autem dicebant

inbelsebud inprincipe demoniorum

eicit demones

Circumibat hs ciuitates omnes

& castella. docens insinagogis eorum

& praedicans euangelium regni & curans

omnem languorem & omnem infirmitate.

Videns autem turbas misertus est eis

quia erant uexati & iacentes sicut oues

non habentes pastorem

Tunc dicit discipulis suis messis qui

dem multa. operarii autem pauci rogate

ergo dnm messis ut eiciat operarios

in messem suam

Conuocatis duodecim discipulis

suis dedit eis potestatem spm immundo

rum ut eicerent eos & curarent omne

32

suam & sequitur me nonest medignus:

Uniuenit animam suam perdet

illam · & quiperdiderit animam

suam propterme inueniet eam :

Uireaperit uos mereapit & qui

mereapit recapiteum quime misit:

Uireapit prophetam innomine

prophete · mercadem prophete

accapiet · & quireapit iustum innomine

iusti mercadem iusti accapis— :

Quicumque potum dederit uni

exminimis istis calicem aquae fri

gidae tantum innomine discipuli amen

dicouobis nonperos— mercadem suam:

Factum est cum consummasse

ihs uerba haec praecipiens duo

decim discipulis suis transiit inde ut

sabbatis benefacere·:·

Tuncait homini extende manum

tuam extendit & restituta est sanui

a sicut altera·:·

Euntes autem farissei consiliū

faciebant adversus eum quomo

do eum perderent·:·

hs auttem sciens secessit inde·& secu

tisunt eum multa & curauiteos om

nes & praecipit eis nemanifestum eum

facerent utadimpleretur quod dictum

est peressaiam profetam dicentem

Ecce puer meus quem elegi dilectusmes

inquobene conplacuit animaemeae ponā

spiritumeum supereum & iudicium gentibus nuntiab·

contrauabit noncontendit nequeclama

bit neq; audiet aliquis inplateis uocem

in hoc saeculo neque in futuro :·

Aut facite arborem bonam et fruc
tum eius bonum aut facite arborem ma
lam et fructum eius malum siquidem
ex fructu arbor. cognoscitur progenies
uiperarum quomodo potestis bona lo
qui cum sitis mali · ex abundantia enim
cordis os loquitur— ·:·

Onus homo de bono thesauro pro
fert bona ·:· Et malus homo de ma
lo thesauro cordis sui profert mala :·
Dico autem uobis quoniam omne uer
bum otiosum quod locuti fuerint
homines reddent rationem pro eo in die
iudicii · Ex uerbis enim tuis iustificabe
ris et ex uerbis tuis condemnaberis :·
Tunc responderunt ei quidam de

64

guierunt eum ut signum de caelo ostende-
ra eis ctalle respondens ait eis

Acto uespere dicitis serenum erit
rubicundum est caelu
cum nubibus et mane dicitis hodie t
pestas rutilat enim triste caelum
Ypochrite faciem ergo caeli iudica
re nostis signa autem temporum non
potestas

Generatio mala et adultera signum
quaerit et signum non dabitur ei
nisi signum ionae profetae et relictis
illis abiit Cum uenissent disci
puli eius trans fretum obliasunt
panes accipere

Qui dixit eis intendite uobis et ca
uete a fermento phariseorum

ɛt saddu caeorum ::

Alii cogitabant interse dicentes
quia panes nonaccipimus :: Sciens
autem ihs cogitationes eorum dixit
quid cogitatis intervos modicae fidei
quia panes nonhabetis nondum intel
legitis neque· recordamini deguinq;
panibus ɛquinque· milibus hominum
ɛquod cofphinos sumpsistis neque·
septem panes ɛquattuor miliae
minum ɛquod sportas sumpsistis·
quare· nonintellegitis quianondepa
ne· dixi uobis cauete· afermento sa
ducaeorum ɛ pharissaeorum ::
Tunc intellexerunt quianondepani
bus dixerit cauete· afermento pani
um pharisseorum ɛsaddouccaeorū

37

Et confestim uiderunt Et secuta sunt eu(m)

L·XXI· Cum adpropinquasse h(i)e-
rusolimis Et uenisset in
beth fage admontem oliuea

Tunc ihs misit duos discipulos
dicens eis ite incastellum quod con
tra uos est· Et statim inuenietis a-
sinam alligatam Et pullum cum ea
soluite Et adducite mihi· Et si
quis uobis aliquid dixerit dicite
qui(a) d(omi)n(u)s his opus hab(et) Et confestim
dimitte eos

Hoc autem factum est ut adinl-
pleretur quod dictum est
per aeseiam profetam dicentem dici
te filiae sion ecce rex tuus uenit
tibi mansuetus Et sedens super

assinam & pullum subiugalis

Eutes autem discipuli fecerun
sicut praecipit illis ihs Et
duxerunt assinam & pullum &
inposuerunt super eum uestim
ta sua & eum desuper sedere fe
cerunt · Plurimae autem turbae
strauerunt uestimenta sua inuia

Alii autem cedebant ramos de
arboribus & sternebant inuia

Turbae autem quae praecedeba
nt & quae sequebantur
clamabant dicentes Osanna filii
dauid benedictus qui uenit innomi
ne dni · Osanna inexcelsis ·

Cum intrasset hierusolimam
commotaest uniuersa

Qui autem exaltauerit se humilia
bitur. Et quis humiliauerit exaltabi
tur

Vae autem uobis scribae et pha
rissaei et hypuchritae quiclu
ditas regnum caelorum ante homi
nes uos autem non intratis nech
intro euntes sinitis intrare

Vae uobis scribae et pharissaei
et hypuchritae quoniam comedetis
domus uiduarum occassione longe
orantes propter hoc accipietis am
plius iudicium

Vae uobis scribae et pharissaei
et hypuchritae qui circum itis
mare et aridam ut faciatis unum
prosilitum. Et cum fuerit factus

Ue autem praegnantibus et
nutrientibus inillis diebus :·

Orate autem ut nonfiat fuga
uestra hieme uel sabbato

Erit enim tunctribulatio magna
qualis nonfuit abinitio mun
di usque modo neque fie

Et nisi breuiata fuissent dies
illi nonfieret salua om
nis caro sedpropter electos bre
uiabuntur dies illi :·

Tunc siquis uobis dixerit ecce
hicxps autillic nolite credere

Surgent enim pseudoxpi et
pseudo profetae et dabunt
signa magna et prodigia ita inerro
rem inducantur si fieri potest etiam

104

Eatus ille seruus quem inue
nerit dominus eius sic facientem
cumuenerit ·: Amen dico uobis quo
niam super omnia bona sua consti
tuet eum
Autem dixerit incorde suo
malus ille seruus moram fa
cit dominus meus uenire et coe
coeperit percutere conseruos suos
manduca autem et bibat cum he
bris uenit dominus serui illius in die
qua non sperat et hora qua igno
rat et diuidet eum partemque
eius ponet cum hypochritas illic erit
fletus et fridor dentium
Hic simile erit regnum celorum
decim uirginibus quae accipien

HE
XV.

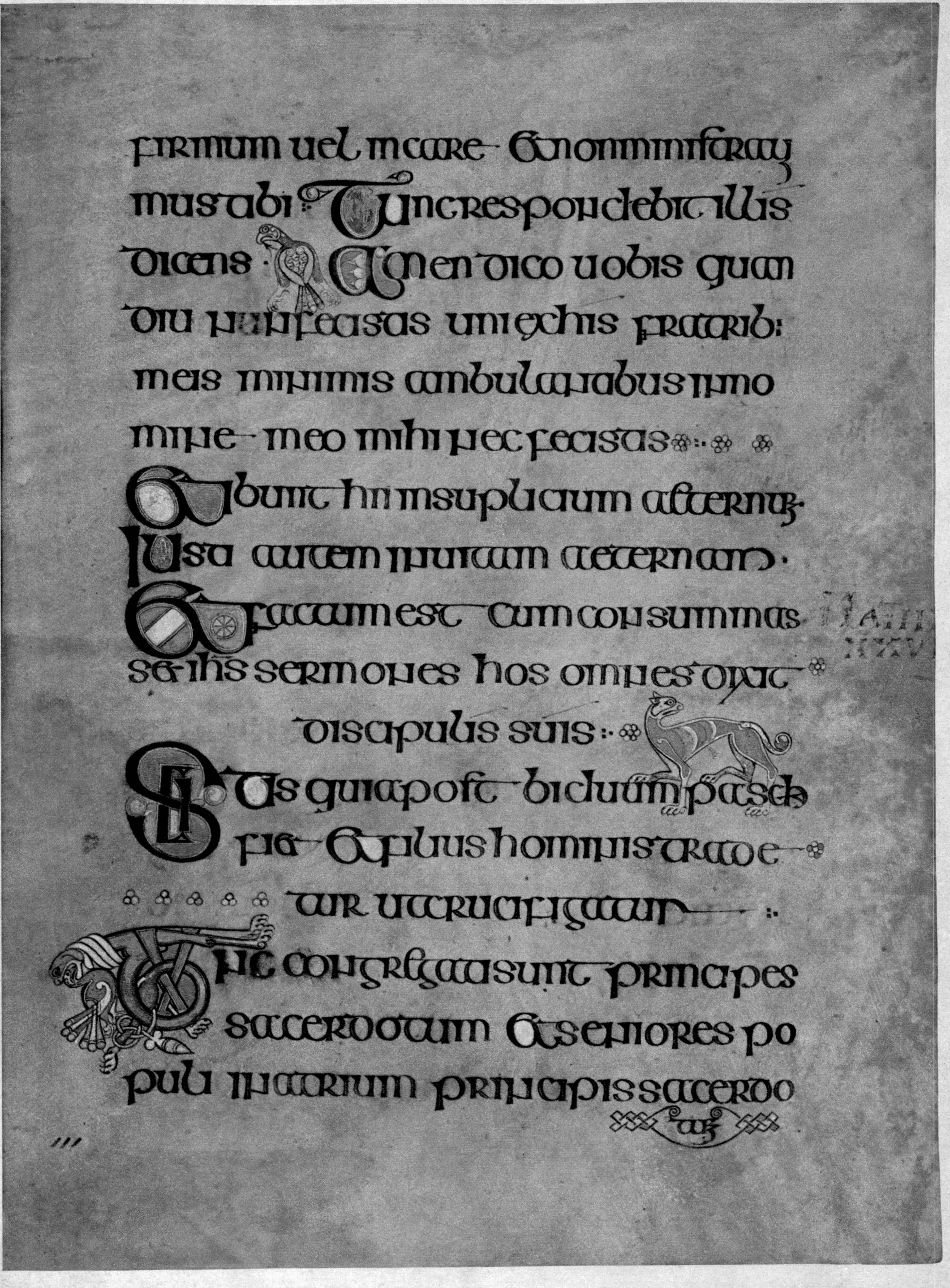

firmum uel micare Gnonminiforan

mustibi : Tunc respondebit illis

dicens Amen dico uobis quam

diu nonfecistis uniexchis fratrib:

meis minimis ambulatabus imo

mirie meo mihi nec fecistis

ibuntt hii insuplicium aeternuz

iusti autem invitam aeternam

factum est cum consummas

setihs sermones hos omnes dixit

discipulis suis

Sus quiapost biduum pasch

fia Et filius hominis trade

tur utcrucifigatur

nc congregatisunt principes

sacerdotum Etseniores po

puli inatrium principis sacerdo

Cenantibus autem eis accepit
iHs panem & benedixit ac
fregit dedit que discapulis suis
dicens accapite edite · ex hoc omnis
hoc est enim corpus meum quod
confringitur pro saeculi uita·
Accipens calicem gratias
agit & dedit illis dicens
bibite · ex hoc omnes hic est · enim
sanguis meus noui testamenti
qui effundetur pro uobis & pro
multis in remisionem peccatoris·
Dico autem uobis qui a non bi
bam amodo de hoc genimine uitis
usque in diem illum quo illud
bibam uobiscum nouum in regno
patris · · & · ·

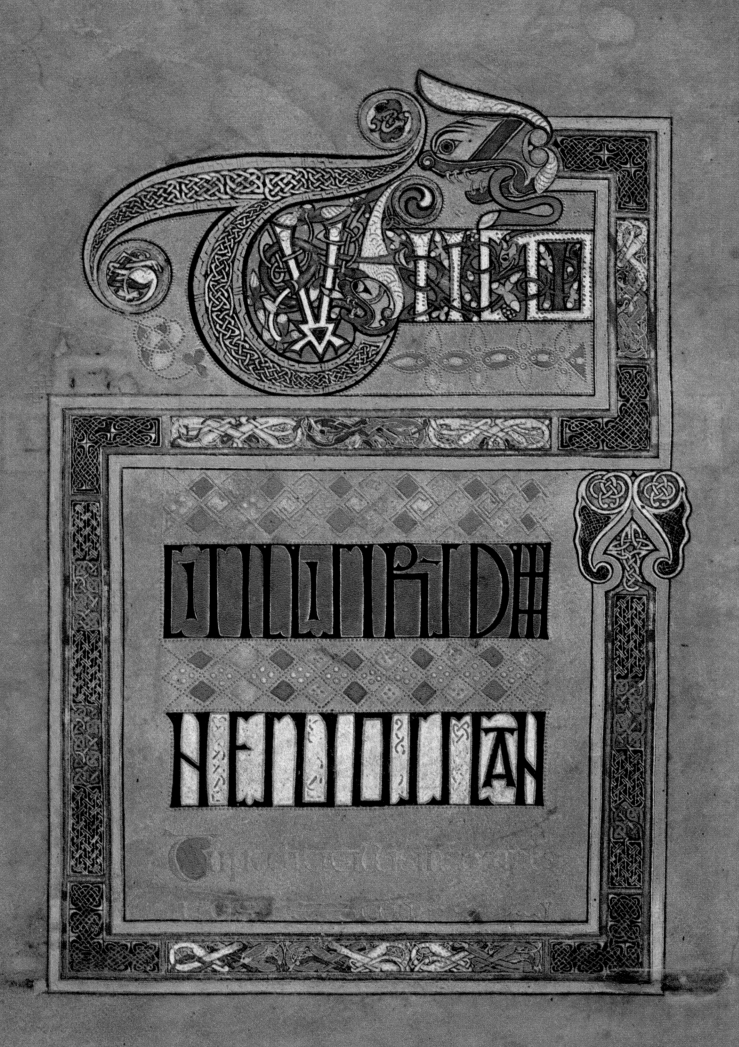

TH. XXViii

**ETBEREI**

sabbata quaelucescit
inprima. sabbata uenit maria
magdalene. & alterta maria uide
re sepulchrum &ecce terrae mo
tus factus est magnus angelus
enim dñi decaelo discendit & ac
cedens Reuoluit lapidem & sede
bat supereum · Erat autem as
pectus eius sicut fultgor & uesti
mentum eius candidum sicut nix·
Praetimore autem eius exterriti
sunt custodes · Et factusuit uel
motan
Respondens autem cat chrisdixta

# MARK

# *Mark*

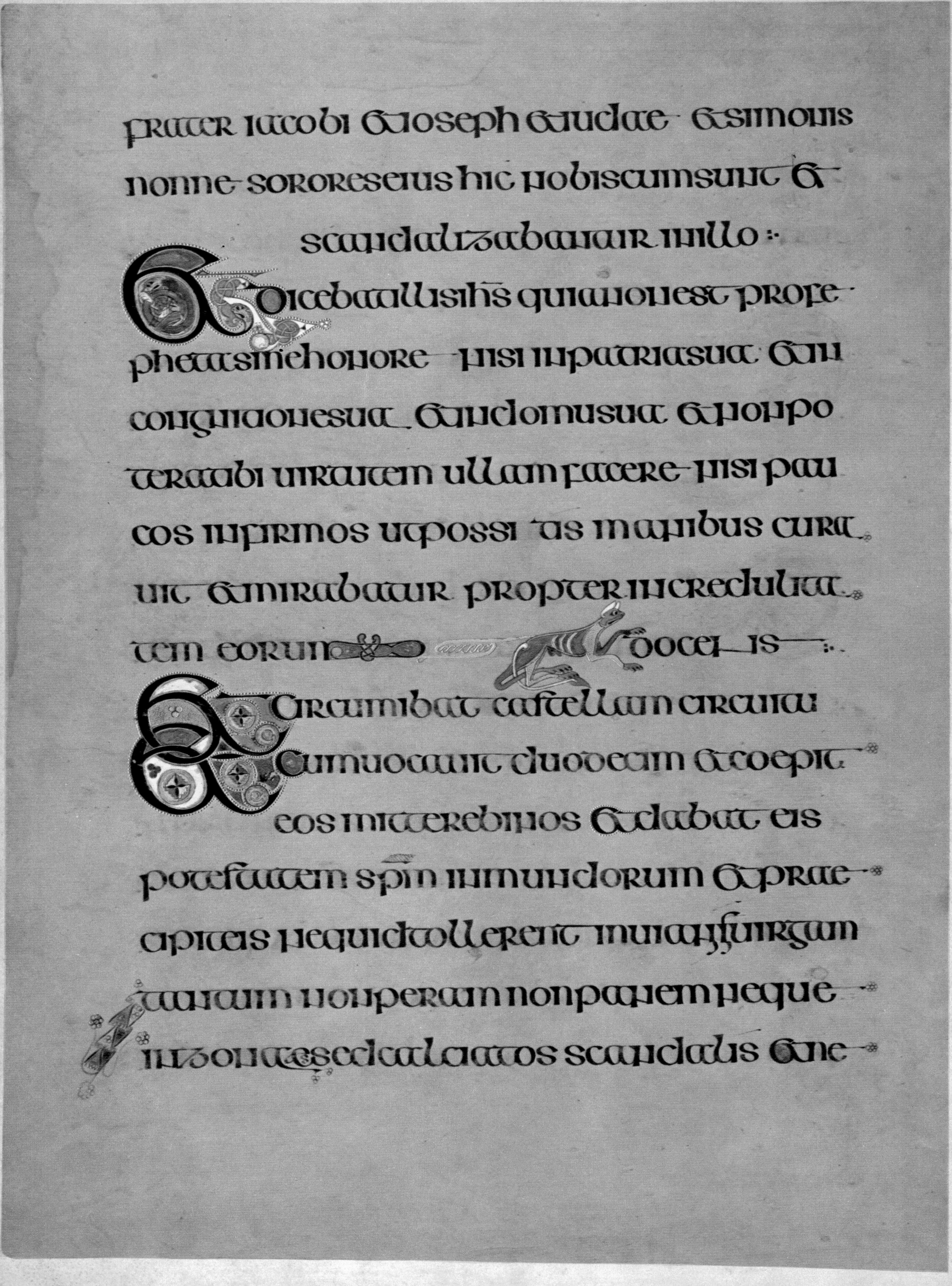

fRATER IACOBI ET IOSEPH ET IUDAE · ET SIMONIS

NONNE SOROReSEIUS HIC NObISCUMSUNT ET

scandalizabantur INILLO ·:·

ET dicebatILLISIHS QUIANONEST PROfe·

phetaSSINEhonore · NISI INpatriasua ETIN

cognationesua · ETINdomusua ET NONpo

teratibi uirtutem ullam facere · NISI pau

cos INfirmos utpossi tas manibus cura

uit ETMIRAbatur PROPTER INCREdulita

tem EORUm DOCEbAs ·:·

circumibat castellum circuitu

ETuocauit duodecim ETcoepit

eos mitterebinos ETdabat eis

potestatem spm inmundorum ETPRAE

cipitas nequidtollerent inuiahsinuirgam

tantum nonperam nonpanem neque

inzonaesodcalciatos scandalis ETne

induerentur duabus tunicis :·

Dicebat eis quocumque introieri
tis in domum illic manete donec exeatis
inde :·

Et quicumque non receperint uos
nec audierint uos exeuntes inde
excutite puluerem de pedibus uestris in
testimonium illis :·

Et exeuntes illi praedicabant ut
poenitentiam agerent Et demo
nia multa eiciebant Et ungebant oleo
multos aegros Et sanabant :·

Et audiuit herodis rex manifes
tum enim factum est nomen
eius Et dicebat quia iohannis baptiza
surrexit a mortuis Et propterea o
perantur uirtutes in illo aliquando

SIS:·

patris nostri dauid ossanna in excel

Et introiut hierusoliman intem

plum & circum spectis omnib:

cumiam uespera essa hora ·:·

exiut in bethaniam cum duodecim

discipulis suis · Et alia die cum ea

rent a bethania cum ai · esurit itaq;

uidisse a longe ficum habentem folia

uenit uidere siquid forte inuenira

in ea  Et cum uenisse ad eam nihil in

uenit praeter folia non enim erat

tempus ficorum & respondens dixit

ei iam non amplus in aeternum quis

quam fructum ex te manduca· Et au

diebant discipuli eius :·

Et ueniunt in hierusoliman

& cum introisa templum

Et crucifixerunt eum & custodieba
nt eum
Erat titulus causae eius in
scriptus Rex Iudeorum
Cum eo crucifigunt duos la
trones unum ad dextris &
alium a senistris eius
& adimpletaest scriptura
quae dicit & cum iniquis de
putatus est
Praetereuntes blasphema
bant eum mouentes capita
sua & dicentes uah qui destruis tem
plum & in trib: dieb: aedificat il
lud saluum te fac ipsum discen
dens de cruce
Similiter summi sacerdotes

inludentes adalter utrum cumscri
bis dicebant alios saluos fecit se
ipsum nonpotest saluam facere
xps rexisrahel discendat nunc
decruce utuideamus &credamus ei
quiameo crucifixi erant
coi iuidebantur ei
facta hora sexta tenebre
factaesunt supertotam
terram usque adhoram nonam
hora nona exclamauit
ihs uoce magna dicen is
helio helio lamasa bcthani quod
est interprætatum dsds meus ut
quid me direliquisti &quidam
decircumstantabus audientes dice
bant ecce heliam uocat iste

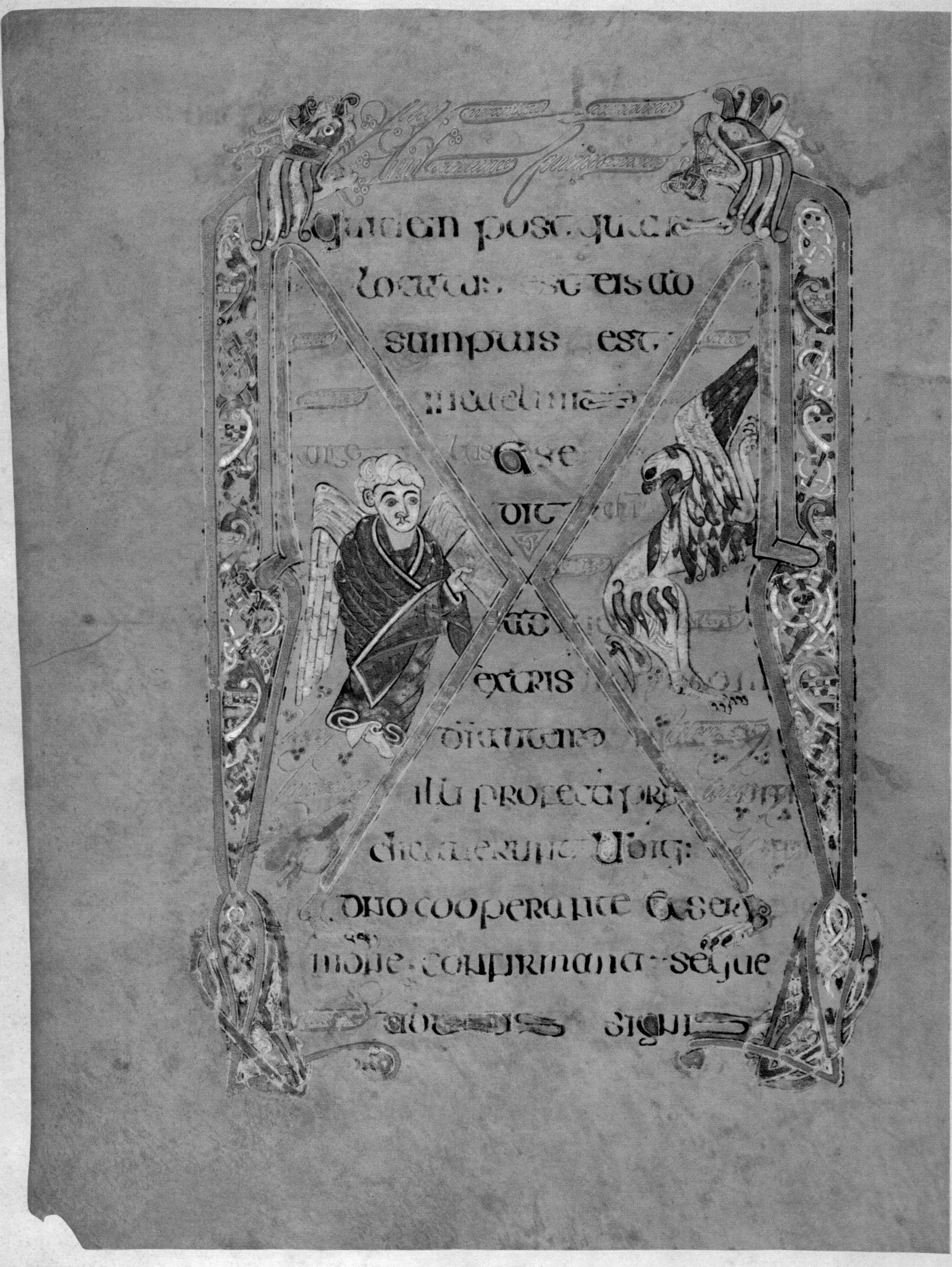

# LUKE

# Luke

quidem multi conatisunt ordinare 7
narrationem quaeinnobis copl̄tesum
rerum sicut tradiderunt nobis qui
a bit nto ipsi uiderunt · Et minis
tri fuerunt sermonis uisum
est · Et mihi adsecuto a principio
omnibus diligenter exordine
tibi obtime scribere theofile
ut cognoscas eorum uerborum
de quibus eructatus es ueritatem

FUITINDIEBUSHEROD

dis regis iudae sacer
dos quidam nomine · zacharias
deuice ania Et uxor illi defilia
bus aaron · Et nomen ei elizabeth

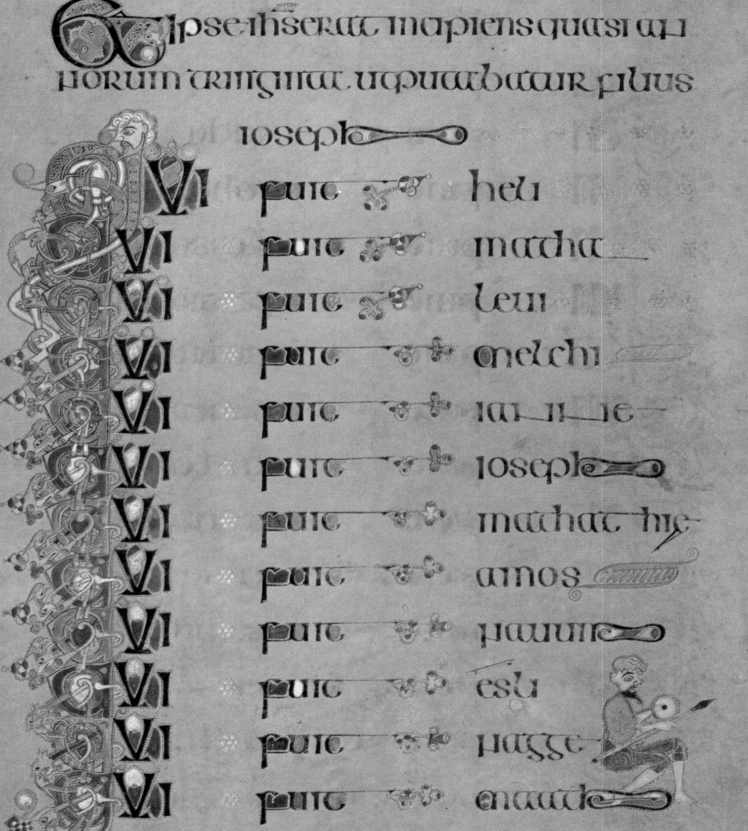

factus est tu es filius meus dilectus in te

bene · conplacuit mihi ·

Et ipse ihs erat incipiens quasi an

norum triginta ut putabatur filius

ioseph

qui fuit heli

qui fuit matha

qui fuit leui

qui fuit melchi

qui fuit iannne

qui fuit ioseph

qui fuit mathat hie

qui fuit amos

qui fuit nauum

qui fuit esli

qui fuit nagge

qui fuit maath

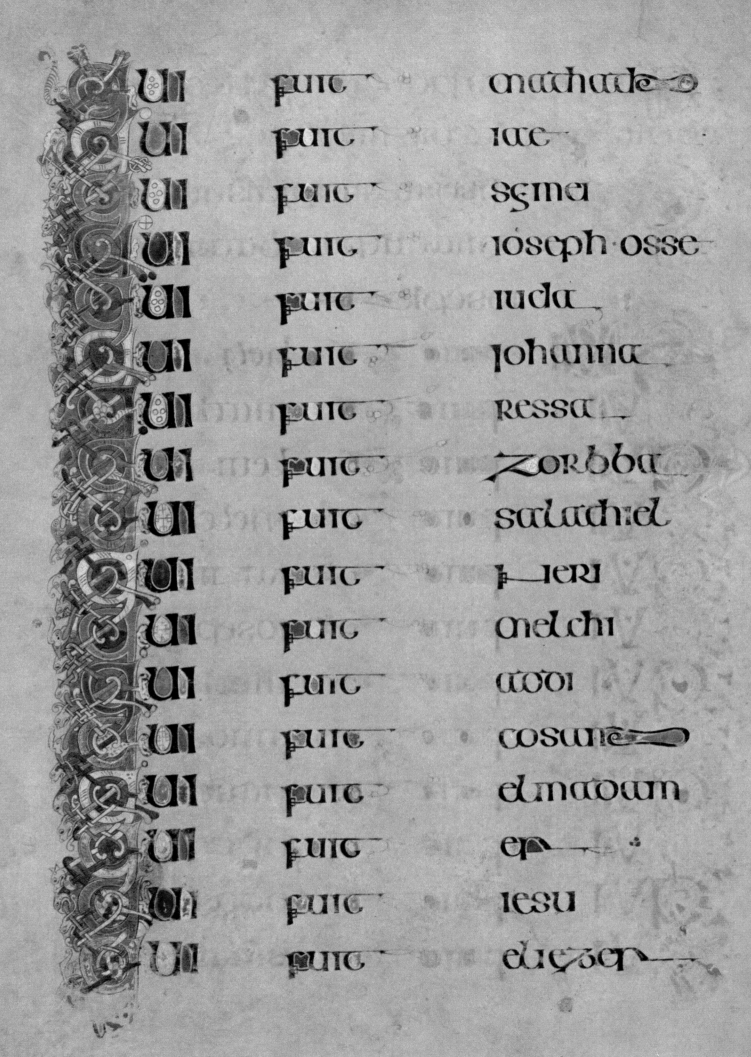

| UI | fuit | enachaath |
| UI | fuit | iare |
| UI | fuit | semei |
| UI | fuit | ioseph osse |
| UI | fuit | iuda |
| UI | fuit | iohanna |
| UI | fuit | ressa |
| UI | fuit | zorobba |
| UI | fuit | salathiel |
| UI | fuit | hieri |
| UI | fuit | melchi |
| UI | fuit | addi |
| UI | fuit | cosan |
| UI | fuit | elmadam |
| UI | fuit | er |
| UI | fuit | iesu |
| UI | fuit | eliezer |

| | |
|---|---|
| fuit | zorin |
| fuit | machat |
| fuit | leui |
| fuit | semeoli |
| fuit | iuda |
| fuit | ioseph |
| fuit | iona |
| fuit | eliacim |
| fuit | melcha |
| fuit | menna |
| fuit | mathachia |
| fuit | nathan |
| fuit | dauid |
| fuit | iesse |
| fuit | obed |
| fuit | boos |
| fuit | salmon |

| | | |
|---|---|---|
| VI | fuit | naason |
| VI | fuit | aminadab |
| VI | fuit | aram |
| VI | fuit | asrom |
| VI | fuit | fares |
| VI | fuit | iudae |
| VI | fuit | iacob |
| VI | fuit | isaac |
| VI | fuit | abracham |
| VI | fuit | thare |
| VI | fuit | nachor |
| VI | fuit | seruch |
| VI | fuit | ragau |
| VI | fuit | faleg |
| VI | fuit | eber |
| VI | fuit | sala |
| VI | fuit | cainan |

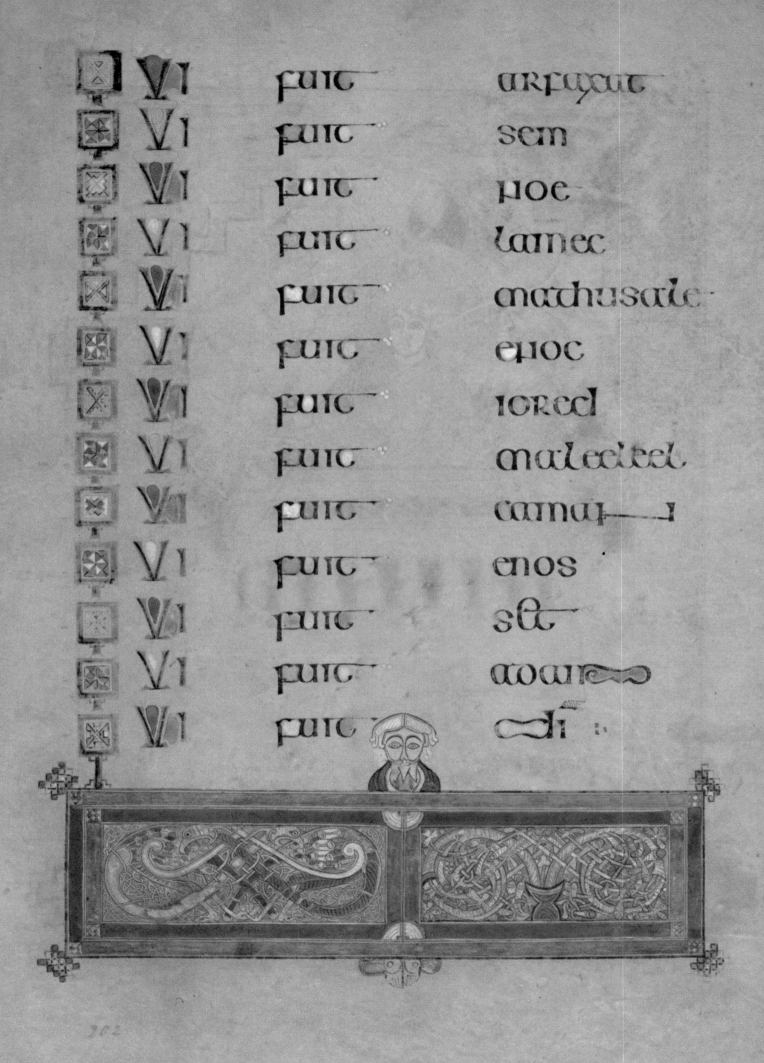

| | | |
|---|---|---|
| VI | fuit | arfaxat |
| VI | fuit | sem |
| VI | fuit | noe |
| VI | fuit | lamec |
| VI | fuit | mathusale |
| VI | fuit | enoc |
| VI | fuit | iored |
| VI | fuit | malecleel |
| VI | fuit | camui |
| VI | fuit | enos |
| VI | fuit | seth |
| VI | fuit | adam |
| VI | fuit | dī |

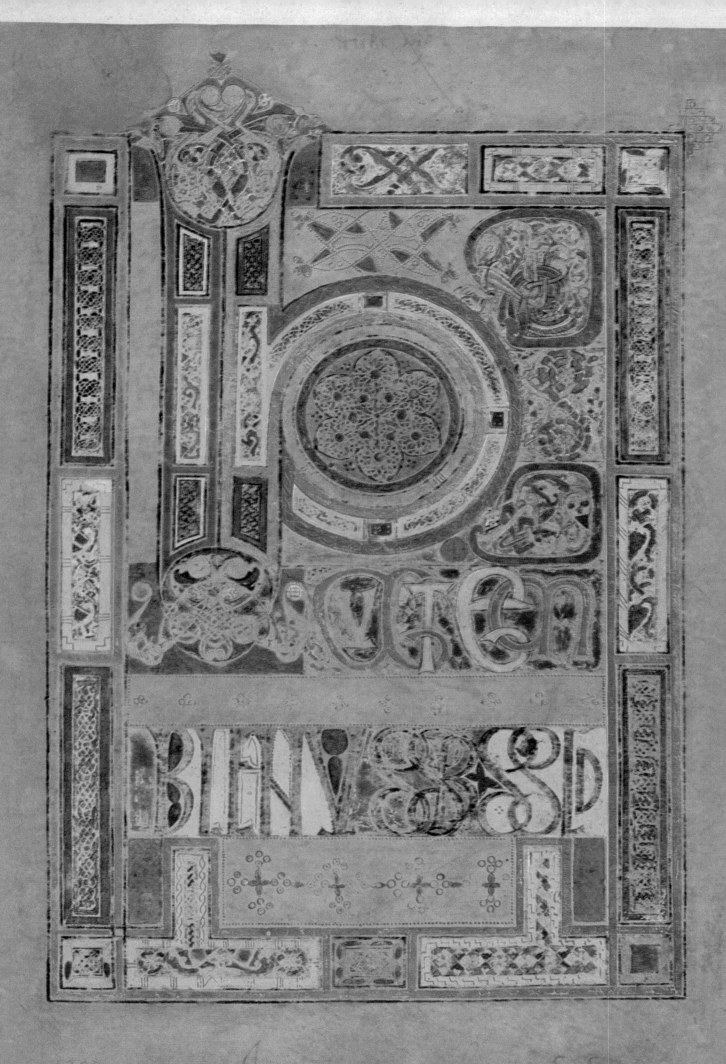

dicit enim uetus melius est ∴

Cum est autem insabbato secū
do primo cum pertransiret ihs
persata uellebant discipuli
eius spicas & manducabant confri
cantes manibus quidam autem phari
saeorum dicebant illis quidfacitis
quod nonlicet sabbatis · Res
pondens ihs adeos dixit nechoc legis
tis quidfecerit dauid cumessurirat
ipse & quicum eo erant quomodo
intrauit indomum dī & panes pro
possitionis sumpsit & manducauit
& dedit his quicum ipso erant quos
nonlicebat manducare · nisi solissa
cerdotibus & dicebat illis quiadnīs
est filius hominis etiam sabbati ∴

omni iudea & hierusalem & transpre
trum & neritima & tyri & sidonisqui
uenerant utaudirent eum & sanaren
tur alangoribus suis & quiuexabant
tur aspiritibus inmundis curabant
tur & omnis turba querebat eum
tangere quia uirtus deillo exibat &
sanabat omnes . Et ipse eleuatis
oculis indiscipulos suos dicebat

Beati pauperes spū quia uestrum
est regnum di

Beati qui nunc esuritis quia satu
ra bemini : Beatus

Beati qui nunc fletis quia ridebi
Beati eritis cum uos oderint
homines & cum separauerint
uos & exprobrauerint & eicerint

& osculabatur pedes eius & unguento

ungebat uidens autem farisaeus qui

uocauerat eum ait intra se dicens hic

si esset propheta sciret utique quae

& qualis mulier quae tangit eum qui

peccatrix est & respondens ihs dixit

ad illum simon habeo tibi aliquid di

cere ta ille ait magister dic duo debi

tores erant cuidam feneratori unus

debebat denarios quingentos & alius

quin quaginta non habentibus illis

unde redderunt donauit utrisque

quis ergo eum plus dilegit responde

ns simon dixit aestimo quia is cui pls

donauit at ille dixit ei recte iudicas

ti & conuersus ad mulierem dixit si

mon uides hanc mulierem intraui

uit dns superfamiliam suam uta

illius intempore triticu mehsuram de

tus ille seruus quem cumuenerit

dns inuenia ita facientem uere dico

uobis quiasuperomnia quaepossidet

constituit eum : Uod si dixerit

seruus ille incor . de suo moram

facit dns meus uenire &coeperit

percutere pueros &ancellas &ede

re &bibere &inebriari uenia dns

serui illius inche quanonsperat &

hora quanescit &diuida eum par

temque eius cum infidelibus pona.

Ille autem seruus quicognouit uo

luntatem dni sui &nonpraepara

uit &nonfecit secundum uolunta

tem eius uapulabit multa. quis

Etqui inmodico iniquus est etinmaio
ri iniquus est si ergo ininiquo mamo
ne fideles nonfuistis quod uerum est
quis credet uobis Etsi inalieno fide
les nonfuistis quod uestrum est dabit uo
bis::
Nemo seruus potest duobus do
minis seruire Aut enim unum odie
Etalterum diliga aut uni adherebit
Aut. uer in comtemp... n potestis do slruire
mamonae
Audiebant haec omnia farisaei qui
erant auuari Etdiridebant illu
Etait illis uosestis qui iustificatis
uos coram hominib: ds autem nouit
corda uestra quia quod hominib: al
tum est abominatio est · ante dm::
Lex etproftae usque adiohan
nem Et exeo regnum di euangeli

...tur & omnis illud uim facit

Facilius est autem caelum & terra

praeterire quam de lege unum

apicem cadere

Omnis qui dimittit uxorem suam

& ducit alteram mechatur & qui

dimissam a uiro ducit mechatur

Homo quidam erat diues & in-

duebatur purpura & bysso &

epulabatur cotidie splendide &

erat quidam mendicus nomine la-

zarus qui iacebat ad ianuam eius

ulceribus plenus cupiens saturari

de micis quae cadebant de mensa diui-

tis sed & canes ueniebant & lingebant

ulcera eius Factum est autem ut

moriretur mendicus lazarus

uatius est illu si lapis molaris inpona

tur circa collum eius & proiciatur in

mare quam ut scandaliz& unum de

pussillus istis

Adtendite uobis si peccauerit in

te frater tuus increpa illum & si

penitentiam egerit dimitte illi

Et septies in die peccauerit in te

& septies in die conuersus fue

rit ad te dicens penit& me dimitte illi

Dixerunt apostoli ad dominum

auge nobis fidem ait autem dominus

Ons si habueritis fidem sicut granum

sinapis diceretis huic arbori mori

eradicare & transplantare in mar

re & oboediret uobis

Quis autem uestrum habens seruum

regnum di · cum obseruatione · neque

dicent ecce · hic aut ecce · illic ecce enim

regnum di intra uos est · Et ait ad disci

pulos suos uenient dies quando desi

deretis uidere unum diem fili homini(s)

Et non uidebitis · Et dicent uobis ecce ·

hic Et ecce illic Et nolite ire · neque sec

temini

Nam sicut fulgor coruscans desub

caelo in ea quae sub caelo sunt ful

get · Ita erit filius hominis in die sua ·

Primum autem oportet illum mul

ta pati Et reprobari a generatione

hac

Sicut factum est in diebus noe

ita erit in diebus fili hominis ae

debant · Et bibebant · uxores ducebant

257

esse · Ipse eni dicit in libro psal

morum dixit dns dno meo sede a dex

tris meis donec ponam inimicos tu

os scabillum pedum tuorum · Da

uid ergo dnm illum uocat & quo

modo filius eius est

Udiente autem omni populo dixit

discipulis suis adtendite a scri

bis qui uolunt ambulare in stolis

& amant salutationes in foro &

primas cathedras in sinagogis &

primos discubitos in conuiuis

Ui deuorant domus uiduaru

simulantes longam orationem

hi accipient dampnationem

Maiorem respiciens autem

erunt autem pestates :⁘

Et ante haec omnia inicient inuobis

manus suas & persequentur om

nes uos tradentes insynagogis & in

custodias trahentes adreges & adprae

sides propter nomen meum contig&

autem uobis in testamonium :⁘

Ponite ergo incordib: uestris non

praemeditari quem admodum

respondeatis egoenim dabo uo

bis os & sapientiam cui non poterunt

resistere & contradicere omnes

aduersarii uestri trademini autem

aparentib: & fratrib: & cognatis

& amicis & morte adficient exuo

bis & eritis odio omnibus homnib:

PROPTER nomen meum Etcapillus

decapite uestro nonperibit inpa

entia uestra possidebitis animas

uestras

Cum autem uideritis circumdari

abexercitu hierusalem tuncsci

tote quiadpropinquauit desolatio

eius

Tunc quiiniudea sunt fugiant

inmontes Etquiinmedio eius disce

dant Etqui inregionibus nonintrent

ineam quiadies ultionis hii sunt

utinpleantur omnia q[uae]scriptasunt

Uaeautem pregnatib[us] Etnutrien

tabus in illis diebus

Erit enim praesura magna

repetanc dies illa tanquam laque

us enim superueniet in omnes quisede

nt super faciem orbis terrae uigilat

Itaque omni tempore orantes ut

digni habeamini fugere ista omnia

quae futura sunt & stare ante

filium hominis

Erat autem in diebus docens in

templo nocabus uero egrediens

morabatur in monte qui uocatur

oliueti & omnis populus manicabat

adeum in templo audire eum

Propinquabat eum dies fes

tus azimorum qui dicitur pasch

Quaerebant principes

sacerdotum & scribae

LVK·XX

uendat tonicam suam ÷ ematgladium

Co enim uobis quoniam adhuc

hoc quodscribtum est oportet

impleri inme ÷ Et quodcum iniustis de

potatus est ÷ Etenim ea quaesunt

deme finem habent

Atrospexerunt dñe ecce gladii duo

hic Atille dixit eis satis est

+ingressus ibat secundum con

suetudinem inmontem oliuarum

secuta sunt autem illum ÷ discipuli

Cumperuenisse ad locum ora

illis orate nentretis intemp

tationem cum iactatis

IPse auulsus est abeis qua

Est lapidis ÷ posita genibus

oRabat dicens :~

ateR si uis tRans fer calicem hunc

a me uerumtamen non mea uo

luntas set tua fiat

pparuit autem illi angelus dece

lo confortans eum & factus est

in agonia & prolixius orabat & fac

tus est sudor eius sicut guttae sangui

nis decurrentis interram

cum surrexisset aboratione :~

et uenisset addiscipulos suos

inuenit illos dormientes praetristitia

& aitillis quid dormietis surgite

& orate ne intreus intemptationem

huc illo loquente ecce turba

& quiuocabatur iudas unus dece

277

ante cedebat eos

Appropinquauit ihu ut osculu
retur eum · Ihs autem dixit illi
iuda osculo filium hominis tradis
Uidentes autem hii qui erat ipsum
erant quod futurum erat dixeru
nt ei dne siuis percuamus ingladio et
percussit unus ex illis seruum prima
pis sacerdotum & amputauit auricu
lam eius dexteram respondens aute
ihs ait eis sinite usque huc
Et cum tetagisset auriculam eius
sanauit eum
Dixit autem ihs ad eos quiuene
rant adse principes sacerdo
tum & magistratus templi et senio

res quasi ad latronem existis cumgla

diis & fustibus cumpraehendere me·

Cumcottidie· uobiscum fuerim intem

plo nonextendistas manus inme· sed

haecest hora uestra· & potestas

tenebrarum

Comprachendentes autem eum

duxerunt addomum principes

sacerdotum

Petrus uero seguebatur eum alon

ge· accenso autem igne· inmedio

atrio· &circum sedetab: illis

erat petrus inmedio eorum quem

cumuidisset ancella quaedam sede

tem adlumen & cumfuisset intuita

dixit & hic cum illo erat At illenega

uit

ubera quae non lactauerunt tunc

incipient dicere montibus cadite su

per nos & collibus operite nos quia

si in uiridi ligno haec faciunt in ari

do quid fiet

Ducebantur autem & alii duo

nequam cum eo uti interficerentur

Postquam uenerunt in locum

qui uocatur caluariae ubi

crucifixerunt eum

& latrones duos unum adextris

& alterum asinistris

Ihs autem dicebat pater dimit

te illis non enim sciunt

quid faciunt

Uidentes uero uestimenta

eius miserunt sortes Et stabat popu

lus spectans · Et diridebant il

lum principes sacerdotum dicentes

alios saluos fecit se saluum faciat

si hic est xps di electus

Iudebant autem ei et milites

accedentes et acetum offerentes

illi dicentes si tu es rex iudeoru[m]

saluum te fac

Erat autem et super scriptio in

scripta super illum litteris

grecis et latinis et ebreis hic est

rex iudeorum

Unus autem de his qui pende

bant latronibus blasfemaba[t]

eum dicens si tu es xps saluum fac

...ana ipsum & alios

Respondens autem alter increba-

bat illum dicens nequetames

dm quidineadem dampnatione

es & nos quidem iuste nam digna fac-

tis recipimus hic uero nihil maluges-

sit & dicebat adihm dne memento

mei cum ueneris inregnum tuum &

dixit illi ihs amen amen dico tibi ho-

die mecum eris in paradiso

Erat autem fere horasexta &

tenebrae factaesunt inuniutul-

sa terra usque inhoram nonam

& obscuratusest sol

Velumtempli sasum est

medium & exclamans uoce

palpate & uidete quiasps carnem & os

se non habet sicut me uidetis habere

& cum hoc dixisset os tendit eis manus

& pedes · AD huc autem illis non

credentibus & mirantibus prægaudio

ait habetis hic aliquid quod manducu

cetur at illi obtulerunt ei partem piscis

assi & fauum mellis & cum manducas

set coram eis sumens reliquias dedit eis·

Et dixit ad eos hæc sunt uerba mea

quæ locutus sum ad uos cum adhuc es

sem uobiscum quoniam necesse est

inpleri omnia quæ scripta sunt in lege

moysi & prophetis & psalmis de me

Tunc aperuit illis sensum ut intellige

rent scripturas & dixit eis quonia

# JOHN

# John

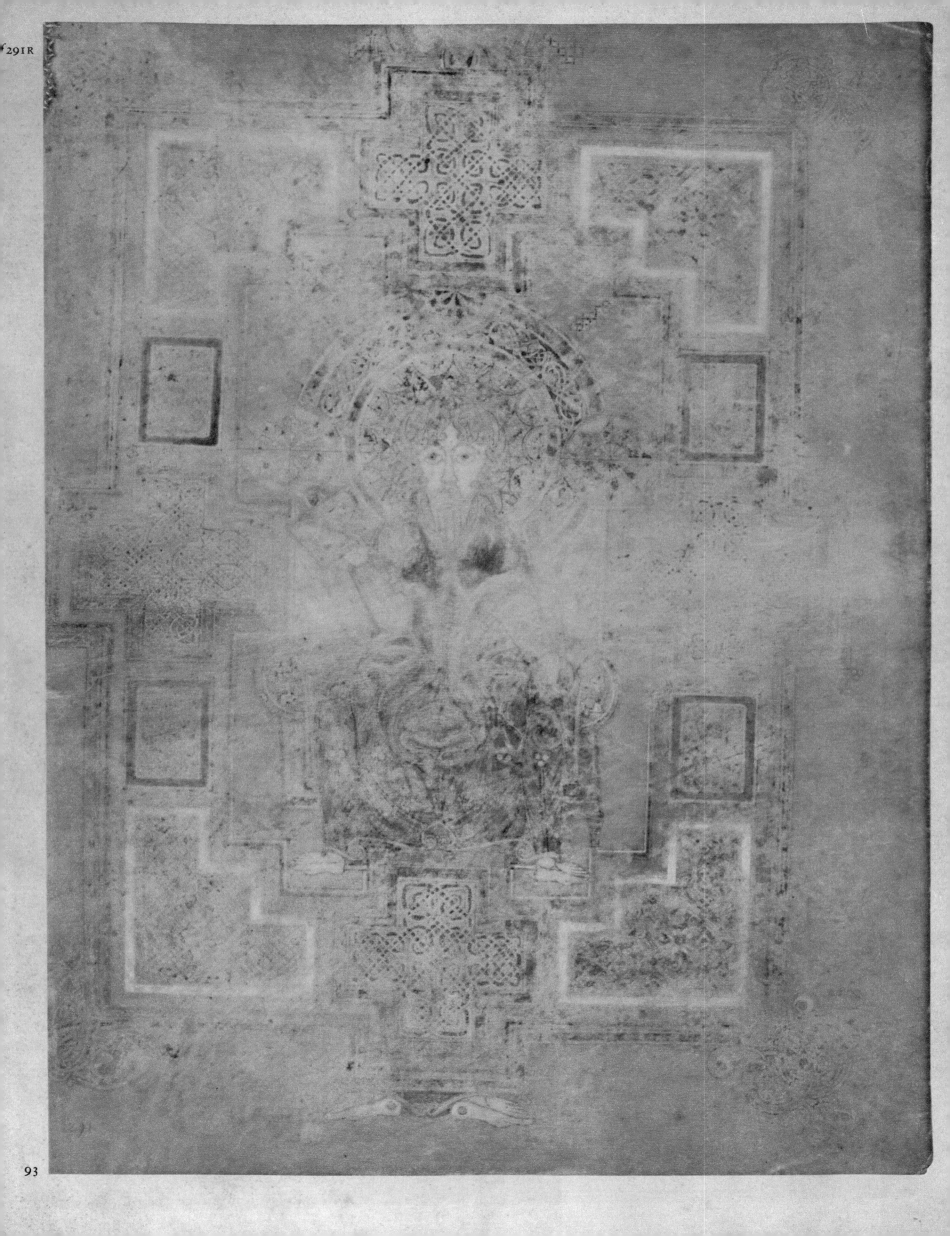

ad eum ut interrogarent eum tu quis es & con
fessus est & non negauit & confessus est
quia non sum ego xps & interrogauerunt
eum quid ergo helias es tu & dicit non sum
propheta es tu & respondit non· dixerunt
ergo ei quis es ut responsum demus his
qui miserunt nos quid dicis de te ipso :·:
Ait ergo uox clamantis in deserto dirigite
uiam domini :·: Erant ex phariseis & inter
Sicut dixit esaias profeta & qui missi fue
rogauerunt eum & dixerunt ei quid ergo
baptizas si tu non es xps neque helias
neque profeta :·: Medius ut
Respondit eis iohannis dicens ego babtizo
uestrum stetit quem uos nescitis ipse est
qui post me uenturus est qui ante me fac
tus est cuius ego non sum dignus ut soluam
eius corrigiam calciamenti :·:

96

Omne quoddatmihi pateraome
uenit— &eumquiuenitnoncicam
foras :· ··· ····· quouoluntatem meam
Uiadiscendi deaaelo nonutfaciam
seduoluntatem eius quimemisit·
Haec estautem uoluntas eius quim
sit mepateris utomne quoddedit
mihi nonperdam exeo sedresusatam
illum innouissimo die· Haecest eum
uoluntas patrismea quimisitme utom
his quiuidit filium &credit meum ha
beat uitam aeternam &resusatabo
eum innouissimo die··· ·····
Murmurabant ergo iudaei deillo
quiadixisse— &osumpanis quide
aaelo disaendi &dicebant nonne hic
estĥs filiusioseph cuiusnos nouimus
patrem &matrem quomodo ergo diat

hicauidicaelo discendi :· murmurare·

Respondit ergo ihs & dixit eis nolite

inuicem nemo potest uenire adme ni

si pater quimisit me traxerit eum & ego

resuscitabo eum innouissimo die · Scrip

tum est inprofetis & erunt omnes doce

biles di omnis quiaudiuit apatre & di

dicit uenit adme :· nisi is quiest

Nonquia patrem uidit quisquam

acö hicaudit patrem :· ·:

Amen amen dico uobis quicredit

inme habet uitam aeternam

Ego sum panis uitae patres uestri

manducauerunt manna indeser

to & mortui sunt:· exipso mandu

Hic est panis decaelo discens utsiquis

ccauerit nonmoriatur— ·:· cendi

osum panis uiuus quidecaelo dis

credentes & quis traditurus esset eum :-

Et dicebat propterea dixi uobis qu
a
nemo potest uehire adme nisi fuerit

ei datum apatre meo exhoc multa discipu

lorum eius abierunt retro etiam noncum

illo ambulabant :- Dixit ergo ihs duo

dcim numquid & uos uultis abire :-

Respondit ergo ei simon petrus dne ad

quem ibimus uerba uitae aeternae :-

habes & nos credidimus & cognouimus

quia tu es xps filius di :-

Respondit eis ihs nonne ego uos xii elegi

& unus exuobis zabulus est dicebat

autem iudam simonis scariothis hicenim

erat traditurus eum cum esset & unus exduo

Posthaec autem ambulabat ihs inga

lileam nonenim uolebat iniudeam

ambulare quoniam quaerebant eu

iudaei interficere :. Erat autem in proxi

mo dies festus iudaeorum scenophegia :

Dixerunt autem adeum fratres eius

transi hinc & uade in iudeam ut & disci

puli tui uideant opera tua quae facis

nemo quippe in occulto aliquid facit

& quaerit ipse in palam esse si haec fa

cis manifesta te ipsum mundo neque eni

fratres eius credebant in eum

Dicit ergo eis ihs tempus meum nondum

aduenit tempus autem uestrum semper

adest parat um non potest mundus o

disse uos me autem odit quia ego testi

nium perhibeo deillo quia opera eius ma

la sunt uos ascendite addiem festum

istum ego autem non tempus nondum in

pletum est

haec cum dixisse ipse mansit

# ENLARGED
# DETAILS

# Enlarged details

The degree of enlargement is given in brackets

f 5R

f 4R

f 5R

f 5R      f 2R      f 2V      f 3V

*f* 4R

*f* 8R

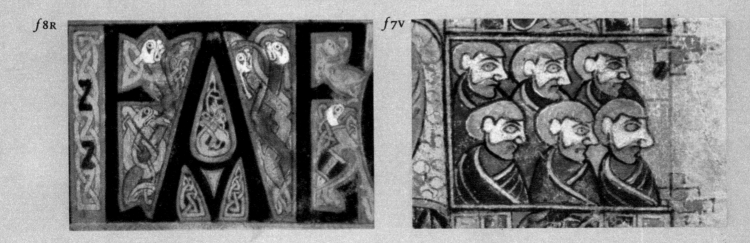

*f* 8R *f* 7V

*f* 19V

f 7ᵛ

f 32ᵛ

f 202ᵛ

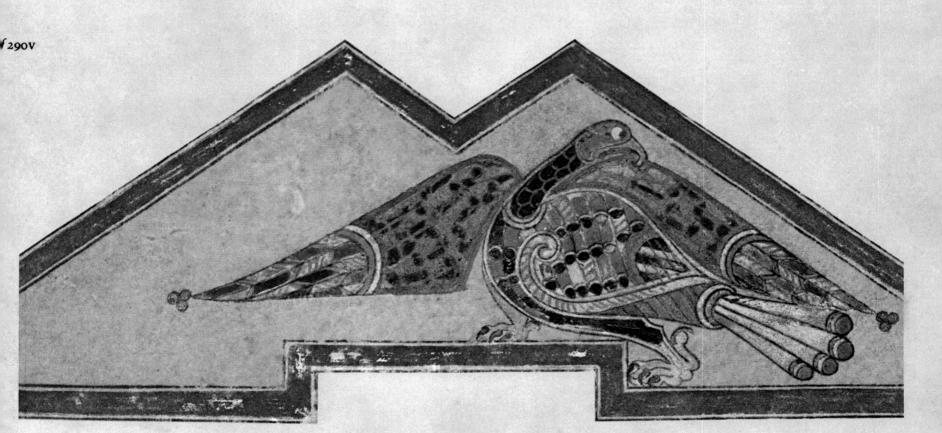

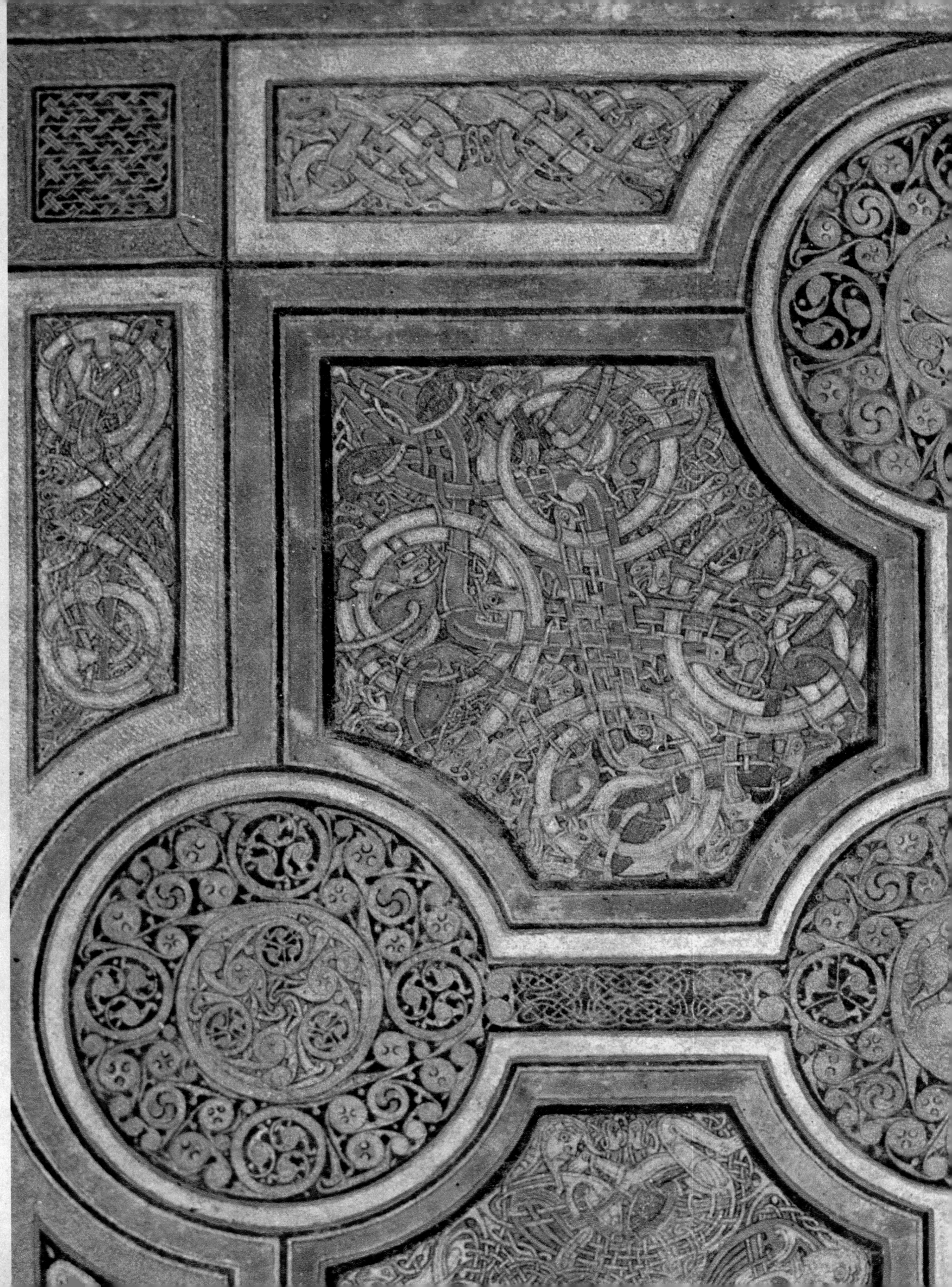

188R

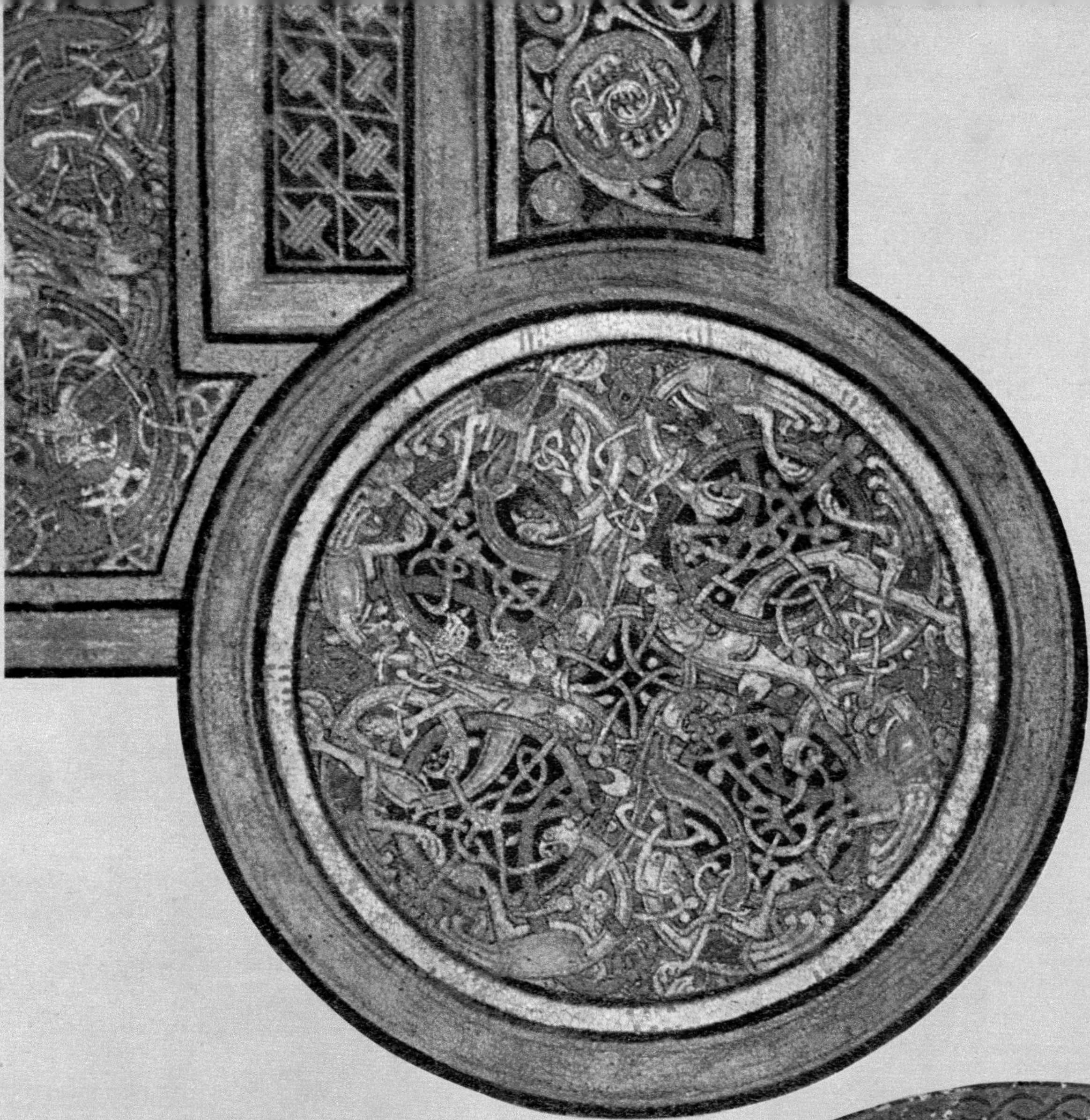

203R

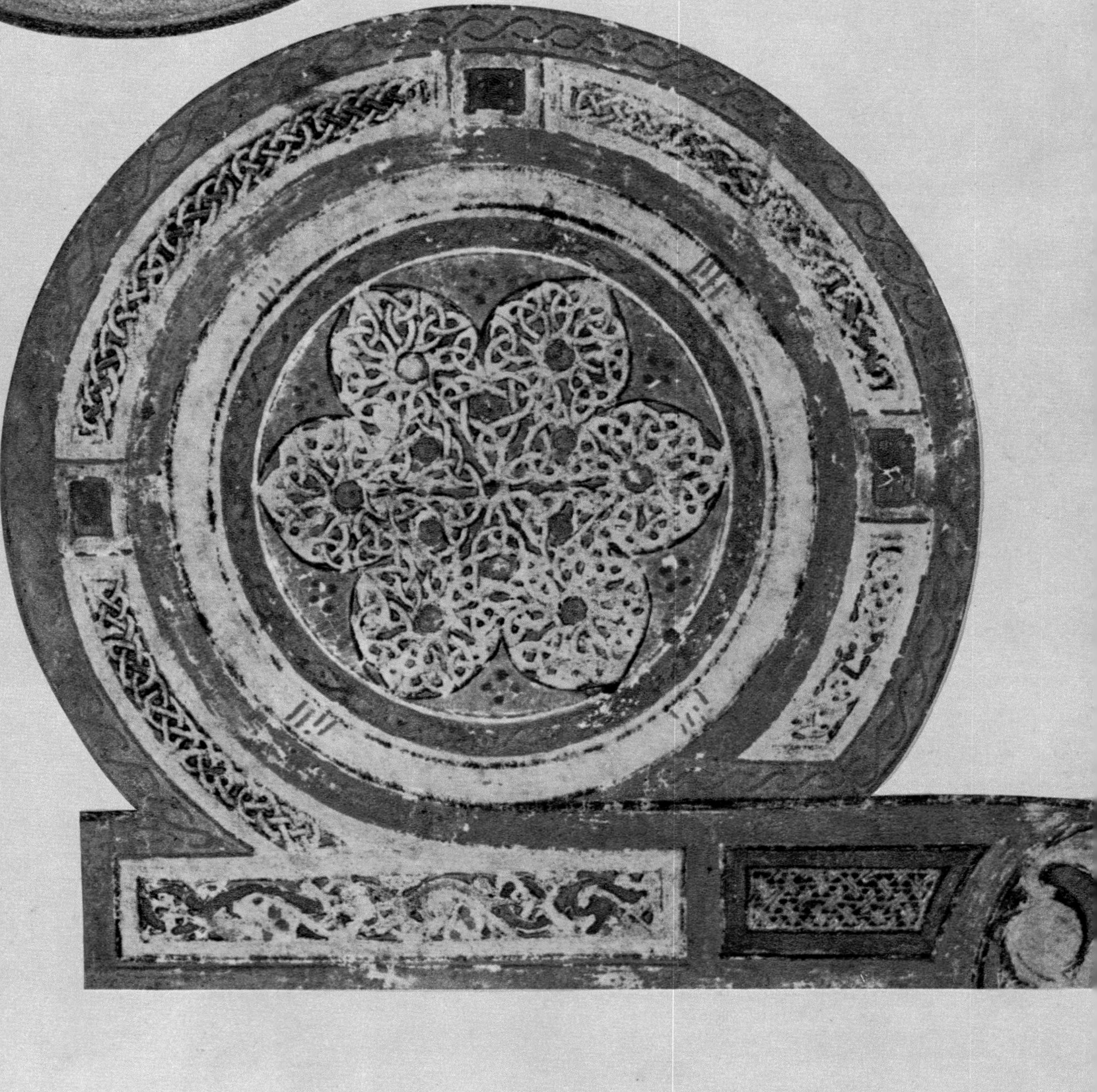

INTERROGABAT E

XPS FILIUS DI

S AUTEM Q

DEBTAS FILI

TEN COETRIS UIR

GE ARCI

NEMO IUNA

TERROGARE

RESPONDENS

INTEMPLO QU

201V

255R

ƒ273R

213R

117

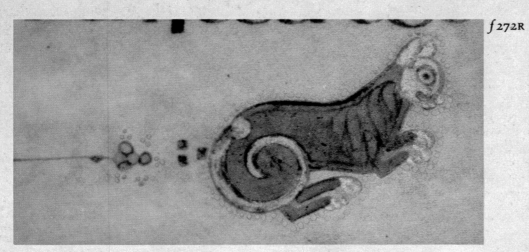

f 272R

f 32

f 243V

f 24

f 230V

118

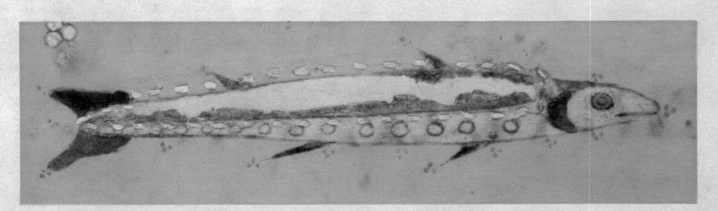

ídíre · quíæauchas&nonau

n auchæparabulam semi

rum · Illisaut

urei &tabut

'o eru

s aut

Hatias

terram

as :

it a hon

a

H

orum :·

t

fretan

&tecte ·:·

mam quam pe

dico uobis

angelis dī

penitentia

ītautem h

duos fūo

et uor ealis

portionen

me contingt

reut euu

Dr

Etue

gua

iubri

Dixerun

ecaudae

cru

que

auc

solyma

Procc

Oraasihs

antequo

sum :· Tle

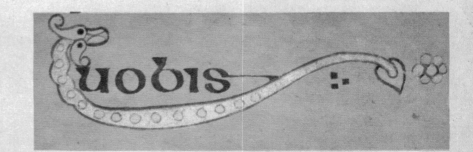

uobis :·

# THE BOOK
## AND ITS DECORATION
*by Françoise Henry*

# Abbreviations used in the Notes

Abbott, *Catalogue*—T. K. Abbott, *Catalogue of Manuscripts in the Library of Trinity College, Dublin*, Dublin, 1900.

Abbott-Gwynn, *Catalogue*—T. K. Abbott and E. J. Gwynn, *Catalogue of Irish Manuscripts in the Library of Trinity College, Dublin*, London, 1921.

Allen-Anderson—*The Early Christian Monuments of Scotland, with an Analysis of their Symbolism and Ornamentation*, by J. Romilly Allen, with an Introduction by J. Anderson, Edinburgh, 1903.

*A.U.*—*Annals of Ulster*, ed. by W. M. Hennessy, Dublin, 1887.

Bieler, *Ireland*—L. Bieler, *Ireland Harbinger of the Middle Ages*, London, etc., 1963.

Brown, *Northumbria-Kells*—T. J. Brown, 'Northumbria and the Book of Kells', *Anglo-Saxon England*, Cambridge, 1972, pp. 219 ff.

Cabrol-Leclercq, *Dictionnaire*—Dom Fernand Cabrol and Dom H. Leclercq, *Dictionnaire d'Archéologie chrétienne et de Liturgie*, Paris, 1907 et seq.

Curle, *Chronology*—C. L. Curle, 'The Chronology of the Early Christian Monuments of Scotland', *Proceedings of the Society of Antiquaries of Scotland*, 1939-40, pp. 60 ff.

*E.Q.C. Cenan.*—*Evangeliorum Quattuor Codex Cenannensis*, Berne, 1950-1, vols. I and II: facsimile, vol. III: text by E. H. Alton, P. Meyer and G. O. Simms.

*E.Q.C. Durm.*—*Evangeliorum Quattuor Codex Durmachensis*, Olten, Lausanne and Fribourg, 1960, vol. I: facsimile, vol. II: text by A. A. Luce, G. O. Simms, P. Mayer and L. Bieler.

*E.Q.C. Lind.*—*Evangeliorum Quattuor Codex Lindisfarnensis*, Olten, etc., vol. I, 1956, facsimile; vol. II, 1960, text by T. D. Kendrick, T. J. Brown, R. L. S. Bruce-Mitford, H. Rosen-Runge, A. S. C. Ross, E. G. Stanley and A. E. A. Werner.

Friend, *Canon Tables*—A. M. Friend Jr., 'The Canon Tables of the Book of Kells', *Medieval Studies in Memory of Kingsley Porter*, Cambridge, Mass., 1939, pp. 611 ff.

Grabar, *Iconography*—A. Grabar, *Christian Iconography*, London, 1969.

Grabar-Nordenfalk, *Painting*—A. Grabar and C. Nordenfalk, *Early Medieval Painting from the fourth to the eleventh century*, Geneva, 1957.

Gwynn, *Armagh*—J. Gwynn, *Liber Ardmachanus, The Book of Armagh*, Dublin, 1913.

Henry, *Irish Art I*—F. Henry, *Irish Art in the Early Christian Period to A.D. 800*, London, 1965.

Henry, *Irish Art II*—F. Henry, *Irish Art during the Viking Invasions, A.D. 800-1020*, London, 1967.

Henry, *Irish Art III*—F. Henry, *Irish Art in the Romanesque Period, A.D. 1020-1170*, London, 1970.

Hubert-Porcher-Volbach—J. Hubert, J. Porcher and W. F. Volbach, *Europe in the Dark Ages*, London, 1969.

*I.H.S.*—*Irish Historical Studies*.

*J.R.S.A.I.*—*Journal of the Royal Society of Antiquaries of Ireland*.

Kendrick, *Anglo-Saxon Art*—T. D. Kendrick, *Anglo-Saxon Art to A.D. 900*, London, 1938.

Kenney, *Sources*—J. F. Kenney, *The Sources of the Early History of Ireland*, New York, 1929.

Koehler, *Karol. Miniat.*—W. Koehler, *Die Karolingische Miniaturen*, Berlin, I, 1930, II et seq., 1958.

Lowe, *C.L.A.*—E. A. Lowe, *Codices Latini Antiquiores*, Oxford, 1935 et seq.

Mâle, *Gothic Image*—E. Mâle, *The Gothic Image* (trans. of *L'art religieux au XIIe siècle en France*), London-Glasgow, 1961.

Masai, *Essai*—F. Masai, *Essai sur les origines de la miniature dite irlandaise*, Brussels, 1947.

Micheli, *Enluminure*—G. L. Micheli, *L'enluminure du haut Moyen Age et les influences irlandaises*, Brussels, 1939.

*Patr. Lat.*—Migne, *Patrologia Latina*.

*P.R.I.A.*—*Proceedings of the Royal Irish Academy*.

Réau, *Iconographie*—L. Réau, *Iconographie de l'art chrétien*, vol. II (nouveau Testament), Paris, 1957.

*Relics of St Cuthbert*—*The Relics of St Cuthbert*, Studies by various authors, ed. by C. F. Battiscombe, Oxford, 1956.

Schiller, *Iconography*—G. Schiller, *Iconography of Christian Art*, I, London, 1971.

Sullivan, *Book of Kells*—*The Book of Kells*, described by Sir Edward Sullivan, Bart., and illustrated with twenty-four plates in colour, London, 1914.

Wessel, *Coptic Art*—K. Wessel, *Coptic Art*, London, 1965.

Werner, *Madonna and Child*—M. Werner, 'The Madonna and Child Miniature in the Book of Kells', *Art Bulletin*, 1972, pp. 1 ff. and 129 ff.

Zimmermann, *Vor. Min.*—E. H. Zimmermann, *Vorkarolingische Miniaturen*, Berlin, 1916.

# THE BOOK

THE BOOK OF KELLS is one of the most splendid Western manuscripts of the early Middle Ages. Its Gospel text is interspersed with large illuminated pages covered with an incredibly fine maze of brilliantly coloured ornaments and with strange, hieratic figures wrapped in the near geometric folds of their draperies. Through the text pages runs the constant coloured arabesque of animated initials made of the bent bodies of fantastic elongated beasts. The student engrossed in the exploration of all these unexpected patterns is soon overpowered by a feeling of both strength and mystery.

It is this very quality of the ornament, the way in which it is used in the manuscript, and its relationship to the text which will be the chief themes of this introduction, whose purpose is to accompany the reproduction in colour of all the large decorated pages in the Book and of many of its text pages and to make them more intelligible. The addition of a series of large details will allow the reader to study many hitherto overlooked patterns and figures which can only be grasped through the help of a magnifying glass when looking at the Book itself.

Controversial matter will be reduced to a minimum. In the last few decades, the Book of Kells and many similar manuscripts have been the subject of violent arguments, chiefly as to their country of origin – Ireland, northern England, Scotland – which have almost overshadowed the study of the books themselves. These arguments will be briefly summarized whenever necessary, for the sake of the reader unfamiliar with them, but, as far as possible, they will be left aside in favour of a purely objective treatment of the manuscript and its decoration. Earlier studies, from the brilliant description of Giraldus Cambrensis and the painstaking count of Ussher to Sullivan's monograph of 1914 and the text of the Urs Graf facsimile of 1951, have already summed up the essential data of this study. They have made my work easier, and I cannot sufficiently acknowledge my debt to them.[1]

## History

Since the seventeenth century the Book of Kells has been in the library of Trinity College, Dublin.

It originally came from Kells (in Co. Meath), where a monastery had been established in the early ninth century, at the time of the Viking invasions, by the monks of the monastery

---

1. The Book of Kells has been discussed, and some of its pages illustrated since the middle of the nineteenth century: J. O. Westwood, *Palaeographia Sacra Pictoria*, London, 1843, and *Facsimiles of Miniatures and Ornaments in Anglo-Saxon and Irish Manuscripts*, London, 1868; J. H. Todd, 'Remarks on Illumination in some Irish Biblical manuscripts', *Vetusta Monumenta*, (Society of Antiquaries, London), VI, 1869; *Palaeographical Society Facsimiles*, London, pls. 55–58 and 88–89; T. J. Gilbert, *Facsimiles of National Manuscripts of Ireland*, Southampton, 1874 et seq., vol. I, pp. IX–XII, 12–21, pls. VI–XVII; T. K. Abbott, *Celtic Ornaments from the Book of Kells*, London, 1895; S. F. N. Robinson, *Celtic Illuminative Art in the Gospel-books of Durrow, Lindisfarne and Kells*, Dublin, 1908; J. A. Herbert, *Illuminated Manuscripts*, London, 1911. Most of the large miniatures were published and the text discussed at length in *The Book of Kells*, described by Sir Edward Sullivan, Bart., and illustrated with twenty-four plates in colour, London, 1914. A complete facsimile, with the miniatures reproduced in colour and most of the text pages in black, is found in *Evangeliorum Quattuor Codex Cenannensis*, Berne, 1950–51, vols. I and II, facsimile; vol. III, text, by E. H. Alton, P. Meyer and G. O. Simms. Two small books give a selection of photographs and a short study: G. O. Simms, *The Book of Kells*, Dublin, 1961; J. J. Sweeney, *Irish Illuminated Manuscripts*, UNESCO, 1965.
See the relevant notices in various repertories: E. H. Zimmermann, *Vorkarolingische Miniaturen*, Berlin, 1916, text vol. p. 72, vol. III, pls. 166–84; J. Kenney, *The Sources for the Early History of Ireland*, New York, 1929, 1970, No. 471, p. 640; E. A. Lowe, *Codices Latini Antiquiores*, vol. II, Oxford, 1935, 1970, No. 274; P. McGurk, *Latin Gospel-Books from A.D. 400 to A.D. 800*, Paris, etc., 1961, pp. 81–82.
See articles dealing with some aspects of the Book (apart from those referred to later), chiefly: J. Ebersolt, 'Miniatures irlandaises à sujets iconographiques', *Revue archéologique*, 1921, pp. 1 ff.; A. Clapham, 'Notes on the Origin of Hiberno-Saxon Art', *Antiquity*, 1934, pp. 43 ff.; F. C. Burkitt, 'Kells, Durrow, Lindisfarne', *Antiquity*, 1935, pp. 33 ff.; A. M. Friend, Jr, 'The Canon Tables of the Book of Kells', *Medieval Studies in Memory of Kingsley Porter*, Cambridge, Mass., 1939, pp. 611 ff.; P. McGurk, 'Two Notes on the Book of Kells and its relation to other insular Gospel-Books', *Scriptorium*, 1955, pp. 105 ff.; M. Werner, 'The Madonna and Child Miniature in the Book of Kells', *Art Bulletin*, 1972, pp. 1 ff. and 129 ff.; T. J. Brown, 'Northumbria and the Book of Kells', *Anglo-Saxon England*, Cambridge, 1972, pp. 219 ff.
See also discussions of the Book of Kells in various general publications: Margaret Stokes, *Early Christian Art in Ireland*, London, 1887, Dublin, 1911, 1928; J. A. Bruun, *An Enquiry into the Art of the Illuminated Manuscripts of the Middle Ages*, vol. I (*Celtic Illuminated Manuscripts*), Edinburgh, 1897; J. Brønsted, *Early English Ornament*, London-Copenhagen, 1924; G. L. Micheli, *L'enluminure du haut Moyen Age et les influences irlandaises*, Brussels, 1939; F. Masai, *Essai sur les origines de la miniature dite irlandaise*, Brussels, 1947; A. Grabar and C. Nordenfalk, *Early Medieval Painting from the fourth to the eleventh century*, Geneva, 1957; D. Diringer, *The Illuminated Book*, London, 1958; M. and L. de Paor, *Early Christian Ireland*, London, 1958; L. Bieler, *Ireland Harbinger of the Middle Ages*, London, etc., 1963; F. Henry, *Irish Art*, London, 1940, 1947; new ed. completely modified: *Irish Art in the Early Christian Period to A.D. 800 (Irish Art I)*, London, 1965, and *Irish Art during the Viking Invasion, 800–1020 A.D. (Irish Art II)*, London, 1967; J. Hubert, J. Porcher and W. F. Volbach, *Europe in the Dark Ages*, London, 1969; W. Koehler, *Buchmalerei des Frühen Mittelalters: Fragmente und Entwürfe aus dem Nachlass*, ed. E. Kitzinger and F. Mütherich, Munich, 1972; I. Finlay, *Celtic Art, An Introduction*, London, 1973.

of Iona off the west coast of Scotland.[2] Iona itself went back to the time when the Irish saint Columba (Columkille), fleeing his native land, settled there in the middle of the sixth century. The monastery became a missionary centre to the population of Irish origin of the west coast[3] and the Picts of the east coast of Scotland, and remained always in close touch with Ireland. It was the headquarters of the Columban community which had many houses both in Ireland and Scotland. When the Viking raids made life on the island too precarious most of the monks moved over to Kells, which inherited Iona's primacy over the Columban monasteries.

It is generally assumed that the book mentioned in a well-known text of the Annals of Ulster[4] is to be identified with our manuscript, and this establishes its presence in Kells in the early eleventh century. In the year 1006 (*recte* 1007) we are told that 'the great Gospel of Columkille, the chief relic of the Western World, was wickedly stolen during the night from the western sacristy of the great stone church at Cenannas (Kells) on account of its wrought shrine.'[5] A few months later, it was found 'under a sod', deprived of its gold. This violent wrenching of the wooden and metalwork covers may well account for the missing leaves at the beginning and end of the Book.

The manuscript was still at Kells when, in the twelfth century, charters concerning property of the monastery were copied on some of its blank pages, according to a widespread medieval custom.[6]

As a consequence of the twelfth-century ecclesiastical reform in Ireland, the monastery of Kells ceased to exist and most of its property passed to the new bishopric of Meath.[7] The old monastic church became the parish church of Kells and the Book remained there. In the early sixteenth century, Gerald Plunkett of Dublin wrote in it the numbers of the chapters of the Gospels according to the division established in the thirteenth century by Stephen Langton. In 1621 James Ussher, then bishop-elect of Meath, counted the leaves and wrote his findings in the Book.

In 1654, the Cromwellian cavalry having been quartered in the church of Kells, the governor of the town sent the Book to Dublin for safety. A few years later, after 1661, it was presented to Trinity College by Henry Jones, former bishop of

Clogher, who became scoutmaster of Cromwell's army and, at the Restoration, bishop of Meath.[8]

Whether the Book was at Kells before the eleventh century and whether it was actually written in the monastery's scriptorium are questions which cannot be answered with any certainty. Many solutions have been proposed, ranging over a series of hypotheses: (a) the Book was written in Iona, brought still incomplete to Kells and never finished; (b) it was begun in Iona and completed in Kells; (c) it was written in Kells; (d) it was written and decorated in the north of England (in Lindisfarne?) and brought from there to Iona and then to Kells or directly to Kells; (e) it is the product of some monastery in the east of Scotland.[9] The truth is that we do not know, though the Iona-Kells hypothesis seems to fit most easily with many outstanding features of the Book. It is true that the manuscript is unfinished, but then so are a number of other elaborately decorated vellum books and it would be unwise to deduce too much from such a common feature.

## The background

All we can say with certainty is that the Book of Kells belongs to a distinctive group of decorated manuscripts whose connections are chiefly in Ireland, Scotland and in the monastery of Lindisfarne in the north of England.[10] The group is often described as 'Insular', and though the word is sometimes cumbersome in its vagueness, I am going to use it in this study in order to keep as objective a view of these manuscripts as possible.[11]

Only a few of them are actually dated or signed, but many of them have long associations with monastic libraries in Ireland, Wales, Scotland or the north of England. Some also are connected with Irish or English foundations on the Continent, such as Bobbio, an Irish foundation of the early seventh century, or Echternach, an Anglo-Irish foundation of some eighty years later. The earliest seem to be the Cathach of St Columba[12] (? late sixth century) and some manuscripts from Bobbio[13] of the beginning of the seventh century. Then comes the Book of Durrow (second half of the seventh century).[14] To the early eighth century belong such manuscripts as MS A. II. 17 in the Cathedral Library in Durham,

2. W. Reeves, *The Life of St Columba, Founder of Hy, Written by Adamnan*, Dublin, 1857; *A.U.*, 806, 'Constructio civitatis Columbae Cille hi(in) Ceninnus(Kells)'; see Henry, *Irish Art II*, pp. 7 ff.; H. Roe, *The High Crosses of Kells*, Kells, 1959.

3. When St Columba settled in Iona, a migration from the north of Ireland to the west of Scotland had been in progress for about a century. See E. MacNeill, *Phases of Irish History*, 'The Irish Kingdom in Scotland', Dublin, 1920, pp. 194 ff.

4. *A.U.* 1006; see similar entries in *Chronicum Scottorum*, ed. W. M. Hennessy, London, 1866 (1005), and *The Annals of the Four Masters*, ed. J. O'Donovan, Dublin, 1851 (1006).

5. For the text of *A.U.*, I have followed Bieler's reconstruction of the sentence (*Ireland*, p. 113), which is more logical than the translation given by Hennessy.

6. The charters of the Book of Kells were transcribed by Ussher (*Works*, VI, p. 232); they were published with a translation by J. O'Donovan in *Miscellany of the Irish Archeological Society*, Dublin, 1846, pp. 127 ff.; see Abbott-Gwynn, *Catalogue*, p. 2. For the lost charters, see G. Mac Niocaill, *Notitia as Leabhar Cheannais, 1033–1161*, Dublin, 1961.

7. E. J. F. Arnould, 'Enigmas in the Book of Kells', *Annual Bulletin of the Friends of the Library of Trinity College, Dublin*, 1953, pp. 4 ff.; A. Gwynn,

SJ, 'Some Notes on the History of the Book of Kells', *I.H.S.*, 1954, pp. 131 ff.; W. O'Sullivan, 'The Donor of the Book of Kells', *I.H.S.*, 1958, pp. 5 ff.

8. He had been vice-chancellor of the College. He also gave the Book of Durrow to Trinity College.

9. For (a), see Friend, *Canon Tables*; (b) is the most commonly accepted hypothesis; (c) A. A. Luce in *E.Q.C. Durm*, p. 77; (d) see Clapham, *op. cit.* (above, n. 1), and Masai, *Essai*; (e) see Brown, *Northumbria-Kells*.

10. Lindisfarne had been founded from Iona in 635, then abandoned by its Irish monks in 661, as a consequence of the Synod of Whitby, but remained in contact with the 'Celtic' countries, Ireland and Scotland, for a long time.

11. For a detailed list of these manuscripts, with their library references, see Appendix II, p. 225.

12. C. Nordenfalk, 'Before the Book of Durrow', *Acta Archaeologica*, 1947, pp. 141 ff.

13. F. Henry, 'Les débuts de la miniature irlandaise', *Gazette des Beaux-Arts*, 1950, pp. 5 ff.

14. *E.Q.C. Durm*.

*Fig. 1 Milan, Ambrosian Library, MS S.45.sup. (from Bobbio), initial*

the Echternach and Maihingen Gospels, the Book of Lindis-farne[15] and the Lichfield Gospels. The contemporary Codex Amiatinus, written in uncial script a little farther south than Lindisfarne, in the twin monasteries of Jarrow and Wearmouth, cannot be classified as an Insular manuscript but may have had its influence on the Insular group. To the latter part of the century belong probably the Gospel-book No. 51 in the Cathedral Library of St Gall[16] and the Book of Mac Regol. Then come the Book of Armagh (dated 807–9),[17] the burnt manuscript in the Turin Library, two manuscripts of the Grammar of Priscian and the Book of Mac Durnan which belongs to the middle or perhaps the end of the ninth century.

These manuscripts are mostly written in various forms of what is known as 'Irish script', some in its majuscule, some in its minuscule form. A few manuscripts closely allied to the group by their decoration are written in Anglo-Saxon script, or in some cases in uncial or in Continental script. The Irish script was elaborated in Ireland during the sixth and seventh centuries from various scripts of Roman books brought by missionaries into Ireland from the time of its conversion to Christianity in the fifth century.[18] Later, the Anglo-Saxon script evolved from the Irish and remained very similar to it.

The texts of the Gospel-books belonging to this group are by no means all pure Vulgate. The earlier translations of the

Gospels, the 'Old Latin' texts, were so well known in Ireland and Irish-trained monasteries that they became a strong disturbing element for the copyists of the Vulgate, who often trusted their memory more than the model they had been given. Some at least of the texts of the Vulgate were known in Ireland at an early date, already at the end of the sixth or in the early seventh century, as the Cathach, usually ascribed to that date, has the text of the second translation of the Psalms by St Jerome. So the various mixed versions, including the so-called 'Irish type', must have evolved during the course of the seventh century.

In consequence, the Insular Gospel-books offer a variety of Gospel texts ranging from the Book of Armagh, which is considered as typical of the 'mixed Irish text' and has a considerable admixture of Old Latin or pre-Vulgate readings, to the Book of Durrow, which is a relatively straightforward Vulgate. The Lindisfarne Gospels belong to the same category as the Amiatinus, which presents a remarkably pure Vulgate.

The decoration of the manuscripts of this group fits in with metalwork from Ireland and Scotland, and with the north English and Irish stone crosses and the Scottish carved slabs, all monuments and objects closely inter-related in spite of local variants.

The late stage of development shown in most of its orna-ments and some details of its decoration tend, as we shall see, to mark the place of the Book of Kells amongst the later of the manuscripts enumerated, and seem to date it to the late eighth or early ninth century. But it is essential to remember that such a complex work took of necessity a number of years to complete.

However, much as a manuscript may belong to its own local background, it is related also to the other books of its time. Books are essentially mobile objects, which travel easily over vast distances, primarily on account of their text, but often influencing also ornament and its disposition. In this respect it becomes more arduous to outline the connections of our manuscript, and it is only after studying it in detail that we shall be able to attempt to place it in the art of its time.

*Fig. 2 Dublin, Royal Irish Academy, Cathach, initial*

15. *E.Q.C. Lind.*; I have explained (F. Henry, 'The Lindisfarne Gospels', *Antiquity*, 1963, pp. 100 ff.) why I do not accept the early date (698) for the Lindisfarne Gospels proposed by Rupert Bruce-Mitford and Julian Brown. It will always be mentioned here as a work of the early eighth century (before 721, date of the death of Eadfrith, its scribe and probably its illuminator), and consequently roughly contemporary with the Codex Amiatinus, finished in 716.

16. *The Irish Miniatures in the Cathedral Library of St Gall*, Berne, etc., 1954, text by J. Duft and P. Meyer.

17. Gwynn, *Armagh*.

18. L. Bieler, 'Insular palaeography', *Scriptorium*, 1949, pp. 267 ff.; D. H. Wright, 'The Tablets from Springmount Bog, A Key to Irish Palaeography', *The American Journal of Archaeology*, 1963, p. 219.

## Description of the manuscript

The Book of Kells goes in the Library of Trinity College by the old shelfmark A. I. 6, and is listed in its catalogue under the number 58.[19]

It is a Latin copy of the four Gospels, accompanied by some of the preliminaries usual at the time.

It is written on calf vellum.[20] The quality of the vellum is generally good, but its appearance is very uneven, some folios being thick and nearly leather-like, while others are soft and pliable.[21]

It is a large volume. At present its pages measure on an average 330 × 240 mm (13 × 9½″), but they have been badly clipped by one of the binders and must have been originally about 370 × 260 mm (14½ × 10¼″). This is more than the average dimensions of earlier Insular Gospel-books such as the Book of Lichfield, the Lindisfarne Gospels, Rawlinson MS G. 167 or the Book of Mac Regol, which had a height, unclipped, of from 330 to 350 mm. But even so it fits into this group of Evangeliars fairly well and appears simply as a slightly larger example than most. The St Gall Gospel-book and the Turin manuscript were of a smaller size (about 255 mm in height).

The Book is incomplete. It consists now of 340 folios[22] (680 pages). When Ussher examined it in 1621 it had 344.[23] But already at that time a good number of pages had been lost. Their number can be roughly estimated from the amount of text missing here and there: there is one folio missing after f. 177, another after f. 239 and two or three after f. 330. In addition, slightly more than the four last chapters of St John are missing (from John XVII, 13), which amounts probably to thirteen folios. It is harder to evaluate the loss at the beginning but it may amount to anything between six and ten folios. It seems also that at least three decorated folios are missing: a 'portrait' in St Mark's Gospel, a four-symbols page and a 'portrait' in St Luke. So, altogether, we are deprived of roughly thirty folios, and the whole book must have consisted of about 370 folios, considerably more than the Lindisfarne Gospels' 258 folios or the 169 folios of the Gospels of Mac Regol and the 134 folios of the St Gall manuscript. The disappearance of folios from the beginning and the end of the manuscript is, as we have seen, readily explained by the theft in 1007 and the subsequent tearing off of the jewelled binding and its adjacent pages. The decorated pages may have been abstracted deliberately at some time or other. The others probably got loose from the stitching and went astray as a consequence; the case of one page which was found and inserted again in the eighteenth century is typical.[24]

The Book has been re-bound several times. In the eighteen-thirties a binder clipped the pages severely, cutting into the illumination in several places. The last but one of the bindings was in 1895. This broke down fairly quickly, and when I first saw the Book in the late twenties 22 folios at the beginning were kept loose under separate cover. In 1953 the Book was bound again by Roger Powell. The pages were then very gently stretched so as to bring back to normal flatness surfaces which had developed bulges and glossy slopes. Quires of plain vellum were inserted to allow the perfect balance of the pages and the Book was bound into four volumes corresponding roughly to the four Gospels.

Mr Powell was able at that time to examine the quires.[25] As in the Book of Durrow, they are of varying numbers of folios. Ten (five bifolia) is frequent but by no means the general rule; anything from four or six to eight or twelve appears also. A good number of pages were in single leaves and had been mounted with a slight folding.

The folios of the Book were ruled after folding, sometimes on both sides. Prickings and guiding lines can often still be seen. As we shall see, the number of lines to the page is very variable. In part of the Preliminaries (up to f. 20) it is nineteen, with an occasional eighteen; in the Gospel of St John it is eighteen and in a few cases nineteen. Elsewhere, seventeen is the most common number, but there are variations, generally explicable in terms of text or space. As the problem is closely linked with that of the script, or in other places with that of the decorative structure of the manuscript, we shall have to come back to it again.

## The text

The text of the Book, for the purpose of this study, can be divided into the preliminaries and the Gospels proper.

The text of the Gospels is by no means a pure Vulgate text. Its variants have been listed several times, first by Ussher, then by Abbott in 1884, by Wordsworth and White and recently by Dr G. O. Simms.[26] They are considerable in number and some of them are also of great importance, such as the famous sentence on the Holy Ghost.

---

19. Abbott, *Catalogue*, p. 7; Abbott-Gwynn, *Catalogue*, pp. 1–2.

20. While in the Book of Lindisfarne each calf supplies a double folio with the skin of the spine as the folding, in the Book of Kells the spine often runs across the page. Even if this made it possible to get occasionally more than a double folio out of one calf skin, the number of calves needed would still be in the neighbourhood of 150, a fortune in a society whose economy was based entirely on the ownership of cattle.

21. They have weathered to a variety of shades from the ivory tones of the best-preserved pages to shades of buff and brown, as the coloured photographs show clearly.

22. The folios are numbered in the left bottom corner; there are two consecutive folios numbered 36, so that the last folio is numbered 339 and not 340. There are traces of other foliations.

23. He recorded his count on f. 334v. While engaged in rebinding the Book in 1953, Roger Powell noticed that figures had been written in the top right hand corner of three folios: f. 99 (*recte* 100) is marked 100; f. 196 (*recte* 197) is marked 200 and f. 296 (*recte* 297) is marked 300. These figures may have been inserted by Ussher while he was counting

the pages. That 100 appears on f. 99 is explained by the fact that there are two consecutive folios marked 36 (see n. 22). Between f. 100 and f. 197 there would thus be three pages missing, part of the difference between Ussher's 334 and the present 340. The fourth would be after f. 200.

24. This is the bifolium 335–36; f. 337r has two inscriptions, one (that of Plunkett in the sixteenth century) recording that a fragment of text is missing there, the other announcing: 'This leaf found 1741'. It had been inserted incorrectly, but has been put right in the last binding.

25. R. Powell, 'The Book of Kells, The Book of Durrow, Comments on the Vellum, the Make-up and Other Aspects', *Scriptorium*, 1956, pp. 3 ff. See Appendix I.

26. T. K. Abbott, *Evangeliorum Versio Antehieronymiana*, Dublin, 1884, pp. XXVIII ff.; J. Wordsworth and X. White, *Novum Testamentum Domini Nostri Jesu Christi Latine secundum editionem sancti Hieronymi*, Oxford, 1889, vol. I; G. O. Simms in *E.Q.C. Cenan.*, vol. III, pp. 55 ff.; see also S. Berger, *Histoire de la Vulgate*, pp. 41–2 and 381; H. J. Lawlor, *Chapters on the Book of Mulling*, Edinburgh, 1897, pp. 43 ff.; Gwynn, *Armagh*, pp. CXXXVI ff.

Textual studies of Insular manuscripts have not reached the stage where it would be possible to evaluate the connections of this text of the Book of Kells. It is clear that it differs greatly from that of the Lindisfarne Gospels which have a comparatively pure Vulgate text. But whether it is possible to compare it closely with other manuscripts of the group would at present be hard to say.

The preliminaries belong definitely to two different textual traditions. The canon-tables are the usual introduction to a Vulgate text. They had preceded its existence, as they were established by Eusebius of Caesarea in 320 but they became a regular accompaniment of St Jerome's translation of the Gospels made some sixty years later. They are based on a division of the text itself into sections which should be numbered in the margin for easy reference. Here we come to one of the first major inconsistencies of the Book: though the tables of comparison are given a prominent place, the numbering of the sections in the text has been omitted (except on two pages in the beginning of St John's Gospel), so that the tables are, for all practical purposes, entirely useless. Whether the relevant references would have been added in the margins had the Book been completely finished, or whether, as has been suggested, a fastidious purist decided not to mar the appearance of the pages by their addition, is impossible to decide.

When the Book was complete, the canon-tables were probably preceded by the letter of St Jerome to Pope Damasus explaining the aim of his translation (*Novum opus*), as in the Books of Durrow, Lindisfarne and Armagh. It may also, though this is less likely, have had the letter of Eusebius explaining the use of the canon-tables (*Plures fuisse*), which is found in the Book of Lindisfarne, but not in any of the other Insular manuscripts.

The other preliminary matter is of different origin and goes back to an Old Latin tradition. It consists of *Breves causae*, which are summaries of the Gospels, *Argumenta*, strange collections of lore and legend concerning the Evangelists, and lists of Hebrew names with their interpretation.

The *Breves causae* should correspond to a division of the text into chapters. Like the Eusebian sections, these references have been omitted. But here the reason is different: the *Breves causae* as they stand in the Book are summaries of an Old Latin text and would be hard to reconcile with St Jerome's text. This irrelevance is found also in the Book of Durrow. In fact, the *Breves causae* and *Argumenta* are practically identical in the Book of Kells and the Book of Durrow. The similarity is not only in text, but it extends also to the rather absurd order in which they are presented. Both books start with the *Breves causae* and *Argumentum* of Matthew and the *Breves causae* and *Argumentum* of Mark; then come the *Argumenta* of Luke and John, and then, as a sort of afterthought, the *Breves causae* of

Luke and John. In the Book of Durrow, the misplaced *Breves causae* are at the end of the volume, while all the rest is at the beginning; in the Book of Kells, the series is continuous. Dr Luce has pointed out that the scribes of Durrow and Kells are of one mind when they avoid intruding on the Gospel text by the insertion of the relevant preliminaries at the beginning of each Gospel.[27] In contrast, the Codex Amiatinus, the Lindisfarne Gospels, the Echternach Gospels and the Book of Armagh all treat each Gospel as a separate book with its own preliminaries preceding it. In fact the similarity between Kells and Durrow in this respect is such as to have made Abbott assume that the scribe of Kells actually had Durrow in his hands. This is possible, but it may be also that both scribes used the same model, now lost.

The preliminaries of the Book of Kells include also two fragments of lists of Hebrew names contained in the Gospels, with commentaries and explanations. These lists appear, complete or nearly complete, in the Book of Durrow and the Book of Armagh. In the Book of Kells, the first surviving folio (f. 1r: pl. 1) has the end of the list for the Gospel of St Matthew. Further (f. 26r-v) there is part of the list for St Luke, following the *Breves causae* of John. This hardly makes sense, but not having the beginning of the preliminaries, it is difficult to understand what happened.[28]

In fact, it may be only one example of the extraordinary carelessness with which the text has been handled. The copying has a more than normal share of errors, even by the standards of the time. The treatment of the canon-tables, as we shall see, is unbelievably irresponsible, and if the painters show a great resourcefulness in hiding the errors, they are all the same occasionally thrown off their balance by them. Part of this may be due to faulty models followed too closely, as in the case of the *Breves causae*; but a clever scribe tries to make good the shortcomings of his predecessors. It looks as if the Kells scribe did not care very much, knowing that nobody was going to use the volume for reference, and that it had, first of all, to be a beautiful object.

This is a point which cannot be over-emphasized: the fantastic lavishness of the decoration and the unusually large size of the Book show clearly that it was an altar-book, made to be used for liturgical reading, and probably intended to be displayed open as a sumptuous ornament during ceremonies when pomp was especially required.[29] From this point of view it fits in with the large books of the Insular group written in majuscules, while the smaller ones – Book of Mulling, Stowe St John, Book of Dimma, Book of Armagh, all written in minuscules and of small size – are 'pocket-books' meant for study and easy transport.[30] It is significant that the 'Great Gospel of Columkille' was stolen not from the library of the monastery of Kells but from the sacristy of its church.

27. *E.Q.C. Durm.*, p. 33.

28. There is only about one tenth of the list for Matthew on f. 1r, which means that if it was complete, all written in two columns and in the same script, it would have occupied at least four pages (two folios), not counting f. 1r. There is only one quarter of the total list for Luke on f. 26. So the total list would have occupied three more folios. From the analysis of the quires (see Appendix I), it is unlikely that three folios have been lost between

ff. 26 and 27. There is no trace of the two other lists of Hebrew names.

29. Cf. the Cotton Psalter Vespasian A.I., which was kept on the altar of the Church of St Augustine in Canterbury.

30. P. McGurk, 'The Irish Pocket Gospel-Books', *Sacris Erudiri*, 1956, pp. 249 ff.; F. Henry, 'An Irish Manuscript in the British Museum', *J.R.S.A.I.*, 1957, pp. 147 ff.

## The script

The Book is written in long lines,[31] in a most imposing form of Insular majuscule which includes occasionally some minuscule forms, mostly e and s. The letters are firmly modelled, with thick downstrokes. They are written 'between two ruled lines as in other manuscripts de luxe' (Lowe) and this is emphasized by the treatment of the upper part of the script which follows the top line by massive triangular enlargements of the vertical strokes and a quantity of long, thin horizontal endings. The letters march across the page, deliberate and steady, and would be enough in themselves to make the Book a great work of art.

Lowe notes: 'written by several scribes'. It is certainly possible to distinguish at least three different hands, very close to each other and at times nearly merging into each other. If they are due to three different scribes, which is likely, these scribes were certainly trained in the same school and must have worked in some kind of accord in the same scriptorium. There

are no fundamentally different features, either in treatment of letters or in punctuation, simply a slightly different handling of the same type of writing.

Hand A is found in the beginning of the Book, in *ff.* 1r and 8v–19v (pls. 1 and 12–14) and again in the greater part of the Gospel of St John (pls. 96–100).[32] To this hand is due the most massive and compact of the three scripts in the Book. The letters are definitely lower than those of Hand C. The scribe is inclined to use more majuscule forms and fewer conceits such as superscribed letters. He writes with the brownish gall-ink usual in the West at the time. Throughout his part of the prefaces he uses pages of nineteen lines. In the Gospel of St John, there are eighteen lines to a page, except for *f.* 312 (recto and verso) which has nineteen lines. This scribe feels like an extremely sedate and careful person, not especially inclined to encourage exuberance and fancy in text initials, though in the prefaces he expected a painter to give an elaborate beginning to each of his chapters.

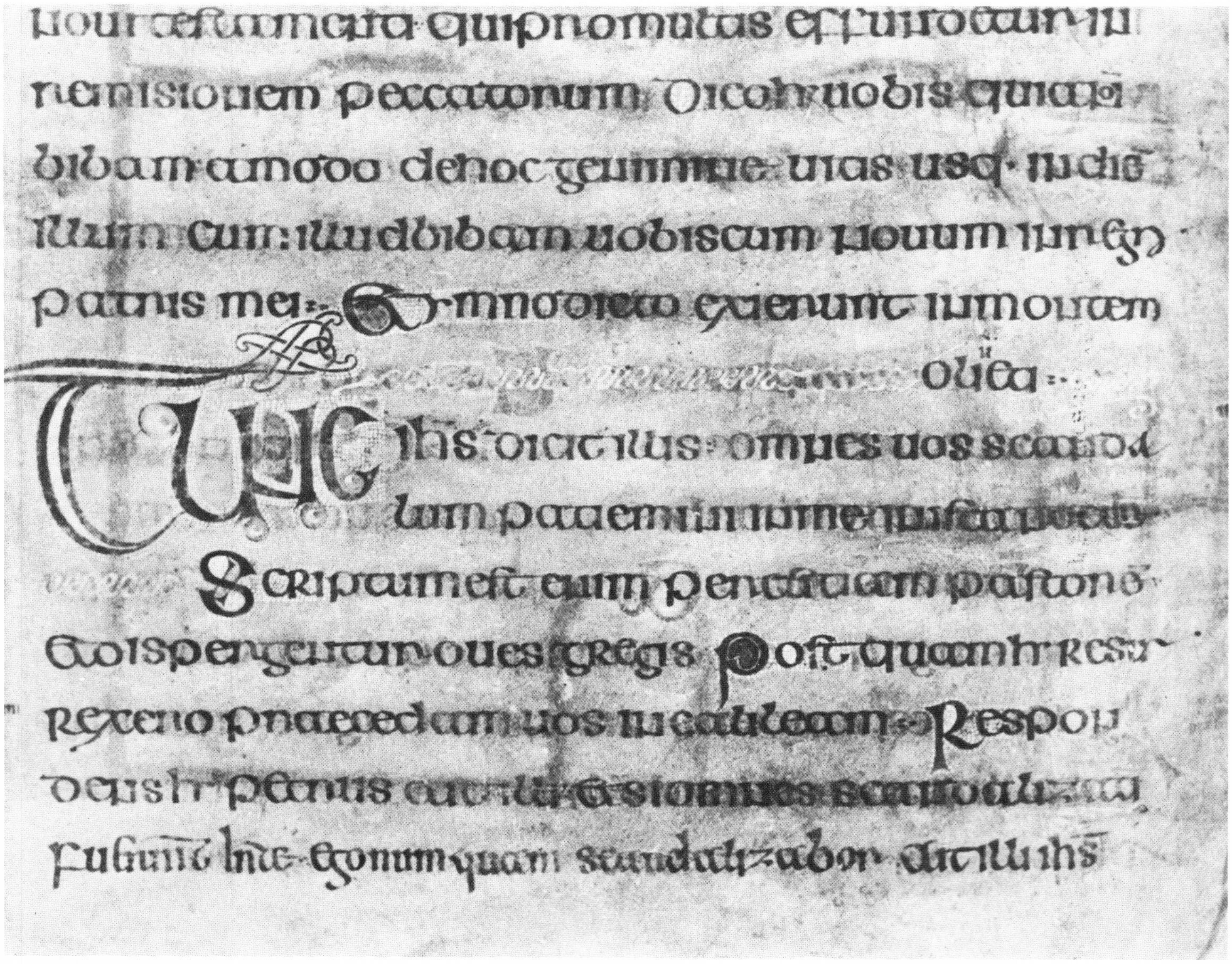

*Fig. 3 Durham, Cathedral Library, MS A.II.17, lower part of a page of text with compressed end-lines*

31. Except four pages of the genealogy in the Gospel of St Matthew, and in appearance only, the two lists of Hebrew names.

32. J. Brown, who seems to assume that the Book is due only to one scribe and who fails to consider the number of lines per page in the last Gospel, says that the preliminaries are purposefully written in compressed writing.

154

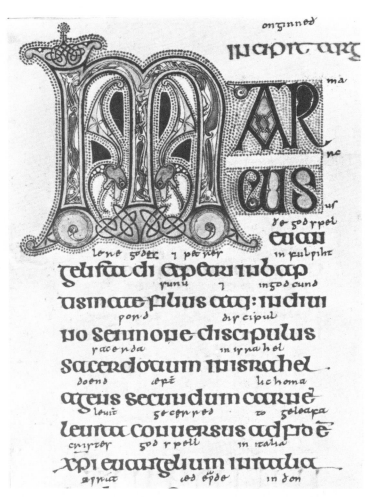

Hand B on the contrary is an extrovert. He starts on *f.* 20r
certainly with an effort at conforming with the preceding pages
as far as the script proper is concerned. But from the start he
uses a brilliant array of coloured inks (pls. 15–18): purple,
red and an intense black made of carbon. Purple ink had been
used by Hand A for the titles of *Breves causae* and *Argumenta*,
but so far it had not intruded into the text proper, and black
ink is a novelty, perhaps indicative of Mediterranean contacts.[33] The scribe is inclined to use more minuscule forms
than does Hand A and most of his end-lines are in a compressed writing suggestive of the appearance of minuscule and
sometimes including minuscule as well as majuscule A.[34]
These lines have very ornamental flourishes of the lower limbs
of letters. Twice, Hand A had used such compressed end-lines
(*ff.* 11v and 12v), but in a constrained and timid way. The
brilliant display of colours goes on until the end of the second
list of Hebrew names. The illuminated capitals in that part are
of a completely different type from the elaborate cartouches of
the earlier prefaces. The *Breves causae* of John start with a
purple and green erect cat (forming a capital I: pl. 17) and the
list of Hebrew names by an A made of large ribbons of
purple with dishevelled snakes as endings. In those few
pages (*ff.* 20r–26v) the number of lines to the page is by no

means constant and oscillates from seventeen to eighteen or
nineteen (pls. 15–18).

The same hand reappears in the last pages of the Gospel
of St Matthew (*ff.* 124ff.: pl. 48) without the previous display
of various inks, but with a title (*Vespere autem*) in the same
style as the I and the A of the prefaces. Though less pronounced,
the tendency to minuscule end-lines is still perceptible.

Hand C is that of the greatest part of the Book. The letters
are slightly higher than those of Hand A, but as this part of the
text is practically all in pages of seventeen lines, the intervals
are hardly smaller. There is something freer in the whole
appearance of the script and perhaps a slight tendency to use
more minuscule forms than did Hand A. But the ink is again
brownish gall. With only one or two exceptions there are no
minuscule end-lines. Except when there is a modification for
decorative reasons, all of this script is in pages of seventeen lines
as far as *f.* 260r where a sudden change to sixteen lines takes
place, which lasts to the end of the Gospel of St Luke (*f.* 289r).
There are certainly differences of height of letters in this part of
the Book. But the treatment of the letters remains so much the
same that it would be hard to attribute them to a different hand.

Here and there, on the reverse of some of the Introductory
pages or of pages of ornamented text, there may be a change of
hand carefully disguised. One such is to be found on *f.* 188v
(pl. 62), the reverse of the *Quoniam*. Though the scribe is
trying to imitate the writing of Hand C almost to the point of
caricature, it seems due to Hand B, and there is a large initial F
in his characteristic style.

The affinities of these various scripts are interesting. None
of them shows a very close resemblance to the tight and slightly
cramped aspect of the Lindisfarne-Maihingen scripts (figs.
4, 26). The work of Hand A has an extraordinary kinship
with the script of the Lichfield Gospels. Though it could
obviously not be the same hand, it is a hand trained in the same
tradition. Hand B, especially in the end-lines, has all the
tendency to decorative writing found in the Book of Armagh.
As for Hand C, when one has allowed for Mac Regol's very
individual idiosyncrasies, such as the slanting backwards of
the letters S and E, his beautiful and free script offers a good
parallel to it, as does the script of Rawlinson MS G. 167, or
indeed the few examples of majuscule script in the Book of
Armagh (fig. 51). But even a later manuscript such as the
tenth-century Cotton Psalter Vitellius F.XI still shows some
kinship (fig. 10). On the whole, it looks as if Script A was a
slightly archaic one, while B and C are more up to date and
have parallels in the early ninth century.

This said, it remains that there is in the script of the Book of
Kells taken as a whole something very individual. It has its
own marked decorative tendencies which include the use of a
number of conceits. For example, the scribe will superscribe
letters which he has omitted in the text, not because he has
forgotten them, nor because he had not quite enough room for
them, but because they constitute an ornament, and in fact very
often they will be the excuse for an embellishment of the text in

---

33. The use of various shades of ink points in the same direction, as it
is a feature of the Codex Aureus in Stockholm, a manuscript partly written
on purple-dyed parchment, like the imperial manuscripts of Constantinople.

34. These compressed end-lines exist on some pages of Durham MS
A.II.17 and in the St Gall Gospel-book, MS 51 (fig. 9).

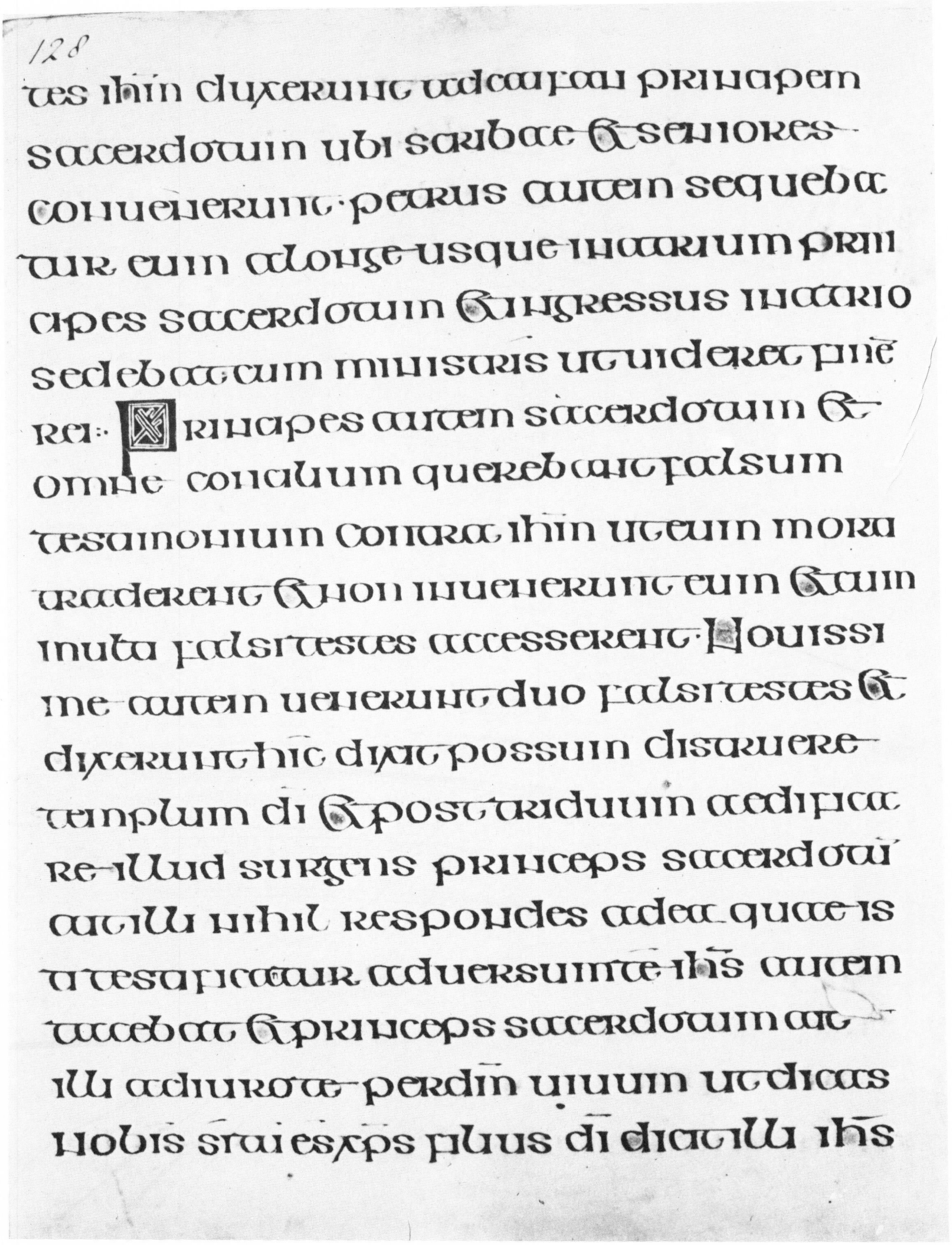

tes ihin duxerunt adcaifan principem
sacerdotum ubi scribae & seniores·
conuenerunt· petrus autem sequeba
tur eum alonge usque inatrium prin
cipes sacerdotum & ingressus intro
sedebat cum ministris ut uideret fine
rei· Principes autem sacerdotum &
omne conalium querebant falsum
testimonium contra ihin uteum morti
traderent & non inuenerunt eum & cum
multi falsi testes accesserent· Nouissi
me autem uenerunt duo falsi testes &
dixerunthic dixit possum distruere
templum di & post triduum aedifica
re illud surgens princeps sacerdotum
ait illi nihil respondes adea quae is
ti testificatur aduersum te ihs autem
tacebat & princeps sacerdotum ait
illi adiuro te perdm uiuum ut dicas
nobis si tu es xps filius di dicit illi ihs

Fig. 5 *Lichfield Cathedral, Lichfield Gospels, page of text* the form of a little animal curled around them. The habit of turning an end-of-line M or N sideways proceeds from the same attitude.[35] The use of what the Irish scribes call 'turn-in-the-path' (*cor fa casan*) or 'head-under-the-wing' (*ceann fa eitil*) becomes in the Book a sort of game, a feat of ingenuity: ends of lines are thrown up or down, as is convenient, and instead of the usual single or double slanting stroke indicating them,[36] a whole crowd of little figures or animals gesticulates directions to the reader (see for example pls. 31, 54). Then there are the drawn-out letters, often filled with colour, which give such a surprising aspect to some pages. M, N or R chiefly suddenly spread over a space big enough for four or five letters or more, elongating themselves into lovely undulating curves.

Corrections are few in the Book, though a great number would have been called for. Whenever they occur, the new letter has been superscribed and a dot in its centre marks the wrong one, but this is rare and it looks as if no corrector had gone systematically through the text. On *f.* 146v a dotted cross acts as a reference mark for two lines at the bottom of the page supplying part of a sentence which had been omitted in the text. Then there is *f.* 218v (pl. 72) whose text is duplicated on the following page. Whether, as has been surmised, it has been cancelled by adding crosses and sprays of foliage in its margins, or whether this decoration of the story of Mary Magdalene so absorbed the scribe's attention that he absent-mindedly started the same text again, is not clear, but I would incline towards the second hypothesis.

## The techniques of painting

The techniques employed by the painters who worked on the Book present some problems which are peculiar to it as well as others which are common to most Insular manuscripts with painted decoration.

Among the general problems are those concerning the implements used by the painters.[37] A quill is usually mentioned, not only in connection with the writing, but also with the drawing of the lines in the illuminations. This must have been used in Kells, but the remarkably even width of lines and especially straight lines in the full-page illuminations may point to a less flexible instrument, perhaps of wood. In addition, the painters were certainly using mechanical aids, such as rulers, set-squares and compasses. Circles drawn with compasses can be seen very clearly on *ff.* 28r and 291r (pls. 21 and 93), but there are many cases when the centres have left no visible trace. It is not impossible also that they used what modern draughtsmen call 'French curves' as these would greatly facilitate the drawing of the irregular curves which seem always to have such perfect balance, as for example in the bodies or wings of animals.

From the very faint outlines of the frame sketched in on *ff.* 30v and 31r (pls. 24, 25) it seems that very diluted ink may have been used for tracing the contours of the patterns, though a stylus or silver-point may have been used in some cases. The painter then filled this in with colour and finally drew the containing lines and the details in the usual gall-ink of the script. In this way, the drawing kept its sharpness.

There is no means of knowing what kind of brush the painters were using, but it must have been a very fine one, coming neatly to a point; marten is the one fur which answers these requirements.

The pigments must have been dissolved with water to which a binding medium, probably white of egg or sometimes glue, was added. The various pigments used in the Book have been studied by microscopic examination with the aid of fluorescent light by H. Rosen-Runge and A. E. A. Werner, head of the Laboratory of the British Museum.[38] The list includes some mineral pigments such as white and red lead,

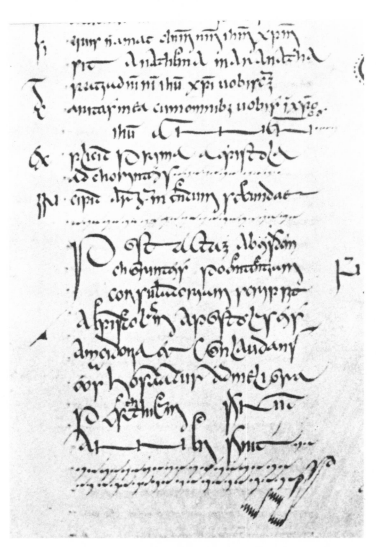

*Fig. 6 Dublin, Trinity College Library, MS 52 (Book of Armagh), details of text*

35. This is of course found in many other manuscripts, but here it is used in a more systematic way.

36. As for example in the *Vita Columbae* from Iona in Schaffhausen.

37. Very little can be deduced from the writing implements represented in the Evangelist portraits. Those of the Barberini manuscript are remarkably well equipped. They hold what seems to be a quill in one hand, and sometimes another object more or less triangular in shape in the other; this may be an eraser. They are sometimes provided with an ink pot tied up to some piece of furniture. Much of this may, however, be derived from late Antique models. See A. Goldschmidt, *An Early Manuscript of the Aesop Fables of Avianus and Related Manuscripts*, Princeton, 1947: Goldschmidt shows convincingly that the objects under the chair of the St Matthew in MS 1395 at St Gall (fig. 11) are rolls of parchment, some of them in a bundle, others half opened, and that they have parallels in 'attributes of the trade' of the deceased on Antique tombstones (pp. 7–8, 31).

38. *E.Q.C. Lind.*, vol. II, pp. 273 ff. This study supersedes earlier ones such as W. N. Hartley in *Proceedings of the Royal Dublin Society*, 1885, p. 485, A. P. Laurie, *The Pigments and Mediums of the Old Masters*, 1914, pp. 70 ff., and J. J. Tikkanen, *Studien über die Farbengebung in der Mittelalterlichen Buchmalerei*, Helsinki, 1933, pp. 216 ff.

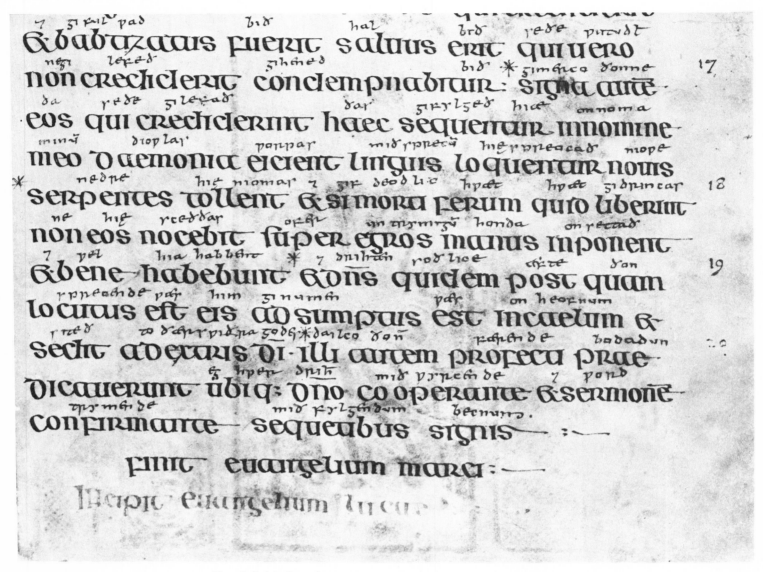

*Fig. 7 Oxford, Bodleian Library, MS Auct.D.II.19 (Book of Mac Regol), page of text*

orpiment (yellow), verdigris (green) and ultramarine from lapis-lazuli (blue) and a good number of vegetable or animal extracts, such as folium (shades from blue and pink to purple), indigo or woad (blue) and kermes (carmine red). These are the colours extensively used at the time, whose preparation is described in several manuscripts, especially that at Lucca (eighth century) or the later writings of the German monk Theophilus (twelfth or thirteenth century). Ultramarine remained during all the Middle Ages the most expensive pigment in existence, ranking with gold in the contracts made with painters. Its price in the eighth century, before the secret of its preparation was transmitted to Europe through Sicily in the twelfth century, was fantastic, as after being imported from the only known source on the confines of Afghanistan, it was submitted to an elaborate preparation by the Arabs who then sold it at the highest possible price. Kermes and folium had also to be imported but were very much cheaper. Locally grown woad is likely to have been used instead of imported indigo (they cannot be distinguished in microscopic examination). White and red lead were probably prepared locally. The green is not malachite, as has often been suggested, but verdigris (basic copper acetate) which is obtained from copper. Some vinegar was generally added to the binding medium in using it, which explains why it eats deeply into the vellum to the point of being visible on the reverse of the page.

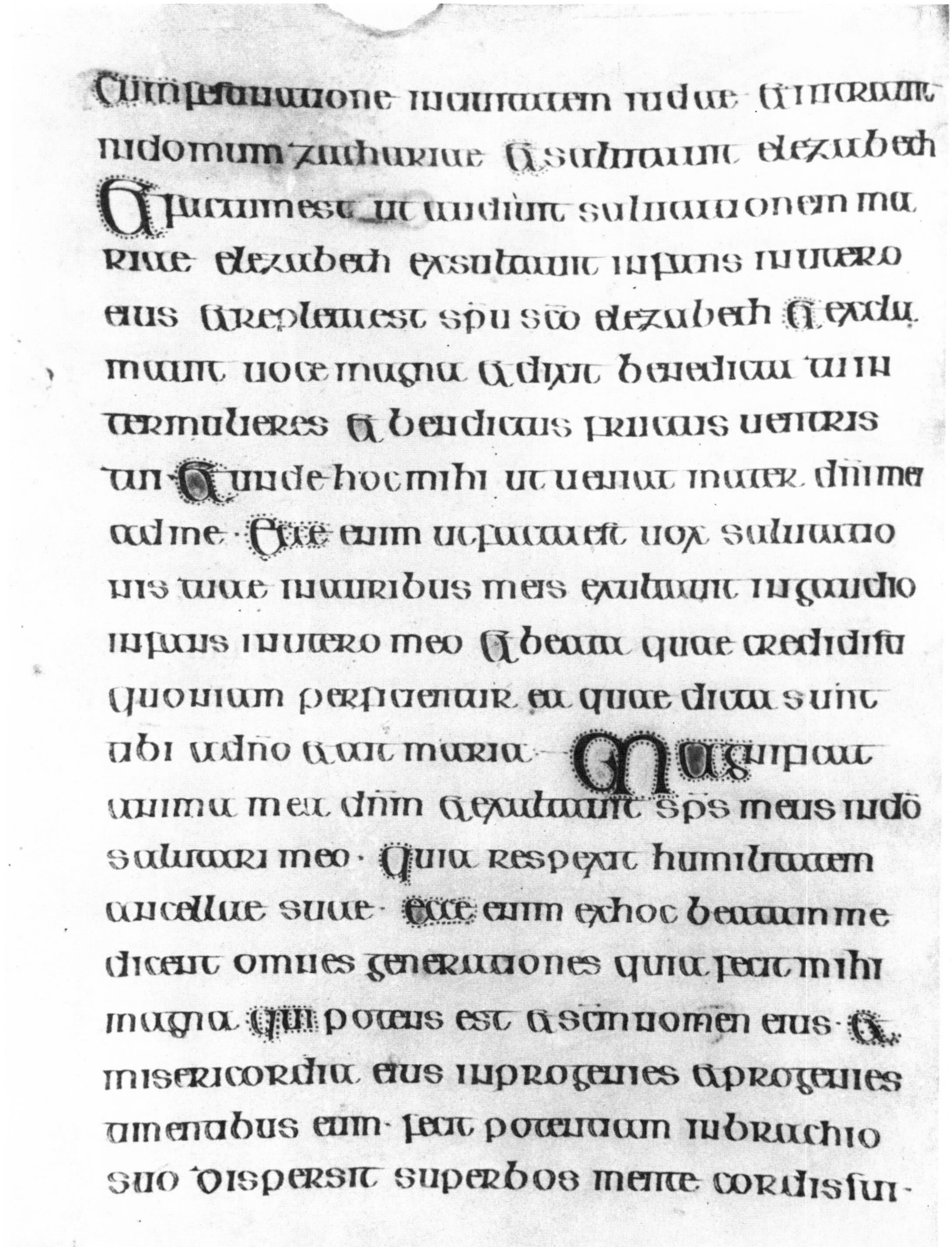

Cum festinatione in montana iudae & intrauit
in domum zacchariae & salutauit elezabeth
Et factum est ut audiuit salutationem ma
riae elezabeth exsultauit infans in utero
eius & repleta est spu sco elezabeth & excla
mauit uoce magna & dixit benedicta tu in
ter mulieres & benedictus fructus uentris
tui & unde hoc mihi ut ueniat mater dni mei
ad me ecce enim ut facta est uox salutatio
nis tuae in auribus meis exultauit in gaudio
infans in utero meo & beata quae credidit
quoniam perficientur ea quae dicta sunt
tibi a dno & ait maria Magnificat
anima mea dnm & exultauit sps meus in do
salutari meo · Quia respexit humilitatem
ancellae suae · ecce enim ex hoc beatam me
dicent omnes generationes quia fecit mihi
magna qui potens est & scm nomen eius · &
misericordia eius in progenies & progenies
timentibus eum · fecit potentiam in brachio
suo · dispersit superbos mente cordis sui ·

*Fig. 8 Oxford, Bodleian Library, MS Rawlinson G.167, page of text*

*Fig. 9 St Gall, Cathedral Library, MS 51, page of text with compressed end-lines*

*Fig. 10 London, British Library, MS Cotton Vitellius F.XI, page of text*

The range of colours in the Book is not the same as that used in the earliest decorated Insular manuscripts such as the Bobbio Orosius and the Book of Durrow. The painters of these manuscripts did not use blue, possibly because ultra-marine was either unobtainable or too expensive. They both used red lead, orpiment, verdigris, white lead and perhaps ox-gall and, in addition, the Orosius has carmine.

The more varied list of pigments in Kells agrees with that of the Book of Lindisfarne and the Lichfield Gospels. But in the Book of Lindisfarne the colours all consist of simple washes of one pigment. In the Lichfield Gospels and the Book of Kells a complicated system of washes of one colour over another develops. In the Book of Kells, for example, ultra-marine or verdigris are found covered by a translucent glaze of folium rubeum, ultramarine may receive a glaze of indigo or verdigris a thin layer of ultramarine. Also the Kells painters make extensive use of white applied thickly as a pigment, instead of reserving the bare vellum as a white as does the painter of Lindisfarne.

The complete absence of gold is one of the striking features of these manuscripts. It is found in only one initial of Lindis-farne. But the painters of the Book of Kells seem especially sensitive to its absence and use the bright opaque yellow of orpiment as a substitute.

*Fig. 11 St Gall, Cathedral Library, MS 1395, St Matthew*

SCS MATHE
EVANGE
US
LISTA

Fig. 12 Vatican Library, MS Barberini Lat. 570, St Matthew

# THE DECORATION

## *General characteristics*

Two outstanding features single out the decoration of the Book of Kells. One is the importance of full-page illustrations. Some of these are 'portraits' – of Christ, of the Evangelists, of the Virgin – each large, haunting, staring at us. But there are also some pages which illustrate a passage of the Gospels, and more seem to have been planned which were never painted.

Full-page portraits of the Evangelists or representations of their symbols are a normal element in the decoration of Insular Gospel-books (figs. 11, 12), found already in the Book of Durrow and the Lichfield Gospels. Illustrations, though rarer, can be traced from the early part of the eighth century. The Codex Amiatinus has a full-page picture of the Apocalyptic Vision which is clearly imitated from some imported manuscript. Durham MS A. II. 17, which may have been in the library of Lindisfarne, has a representation of the Crucifixion whose style is much more definitely Insular (fig. 18). The Commentary of Cassiodorus on the Psalms at Durham (MS A. II. 20) has full-page portraits of David. Towards the end of the century, St Gall MS 51 has pictures showing the Crucifixion and the Last Judgment (fig. 21); a littler later, the Turin Gospel-book has two strange hieratic pages, one of them combined with relevant text, a Last Judgment (fig. 20) and an Ascension (fig. 19). In later Insular psalters,[39] the Cotton manuscript Vitellius F. XI in the British Library and the 'Southampton Psalter' in St John's College, Cambridge, each of the 'Fifties' – the sections into which these Insular Psalters are divided – is prefaced by a full-page illustration of a scene of David's life, or indeed, in one case, of the Crucifixion. From internal evidence those books are likely to belong to the tenth and eleventh centuries. So these full-page illustrations remain a feature of Insular manuscripts over three centuries, suggesting that an existing fashion has only been brought to greater development in the Book of Kells.

The other striking feature of the decoration of the Book of Kells is the profusion of ornament which accompanies the text so closely that only two pages amongst the surviving ones are devoid of it. This decoration consists mostly of initials at the beginning of paragraphs or even in the beginning of some sentences inside paragraphs. But there is also a whole fauna of agile little animals indicating a 'turn-in-the-path', a correction or an addition below the text, or simply filling an empty space.

Decorated initials are frequent in Insular manuscripts (fig. 13), as they are also in pre-Carolingian Continental manuscripts, but nowhere are they so numerous and varied as in the Book of Kells, never do they form such a constant accompaniment to the script. In other books they are added to the text and remain foreign to it. In the Book of Kells they belong to it, grow out of it, mix with it freely. Amongst Insular manuscripts some pages of the Barberini Gospel-book and the abbreviated psalter included in the Prayer-book of Cerne alone show the same intrusion into the text itself of animals and plants, though in a clumsier way (figs. 14, 15).

But in fact we are perhaps at a disadvantage in making comparisons with initials in other Insular manuscripts. The kind of book where a great number of initials is generally found is the psalter, where there is at least one for each of the hundred and fifty psalms, and no Insular psalter of the eighth or ninth century has survived apart from the imperfect psalter in the Book of Cerne. A comparison with the Cotton Psalter Vespasian A. I, an eighth-century manuscript from Canterbury which has strong ornamental affinities with the Insular group, will show immediately what is missing in our information: it has, for each psalm, an elaborate initial often including spirals and little animals (fig. 13), a series which was probably paralleled in eighth- and ninth-century Insular psalters.

Perhaps outside influences also played their part here. There is a group of northern French manuscripts different from most of the contemporary Merovingian and early Carolingian manuscripts which have some kinship with the Insular group. They also show an unusually rich development of decorated and animated initials, and if pages of, for example, the Amiens Psalter (Amiens, Municipal Library, MS 18; figs. 67, 68) are put beside the text pages of the Book of Kells the arrangement of the animals fitting into the shape of the letters is often seen to be practically the same. But this is again a psalter. Other manuscripts, however, show the same tendency, for instance the Sacramentary of Gellone, that perpetual puzzle among pre-Carolingian manuscripts, which is now considered as having been written in the north of France in the eighth century. It too has initials of an infinite variety in which animals and even angels or human figures are bent and combined into letter forms (fig. 69).

39. F. Henry, 'Remarks on the Decoration of three Irish Psalters', *P.R.I.A.*, 1960 (C), pp. 23 ff.

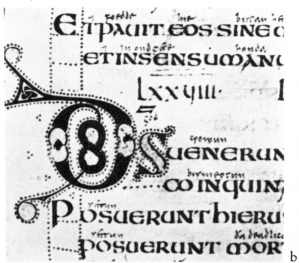

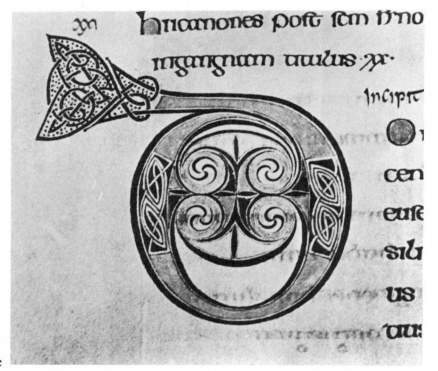

*Fig. 13 Initials: a, f Vatican Library, MS Barberini Lat. 570; b London, British Library, MS Cotton Vespasian A.I; c Durham, Cathedral Library, MS A.II.17; d London, British Library, MS Cotton Nero D.IV (Book of Lindisfarne); e Cologne Cathedral Library, MS 213 (Collectio Canonum)*

164

But whatever its connections, there is no doubt that the Book of Kells towers above all the surviving manuscripts of the same group from the point of view of decoration. In profusion, variety, perfection of minute execution, it leaves them all very far behind. This quality of uniqueness is one of the great difficulties of its study: there is nothing to which it can be compared on a footing of complete equality. One may put side by side isolated features. But for that massive bulk of ornament one does not know where to turn. As far as one can judge from its ruins, the Turin manuscript, though smaller, may have been conceived on the same lavish scale, but its execution was certainly coarser.

A famous passage of the *Topographia Hiberniae* of Giraldus Cambrensis[40] may relate to another book, kept in the twelfth century at Kildare, but if he slightly mixed up his notes it may be a description of the Book of Kells. Enough doubt remains to open up the possibility that another book of the same type once existed. What he says, however, sounds like an inspired description of the Book of Kells:

This book contains the harmony of the four Evangelists according to Jerome, where for almost every page there are different designs, distinguished by varied colours. Here you may see the face of majesty, divinely drawn, here the mystic

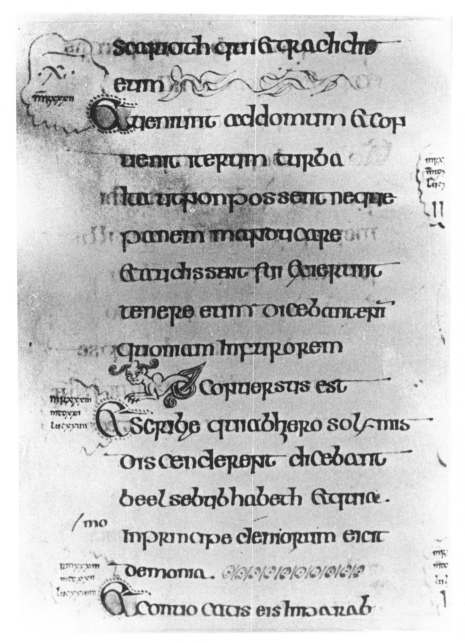

*Fig. 15 Vatican Library, MS Barberini Lat. 570, detail of text*

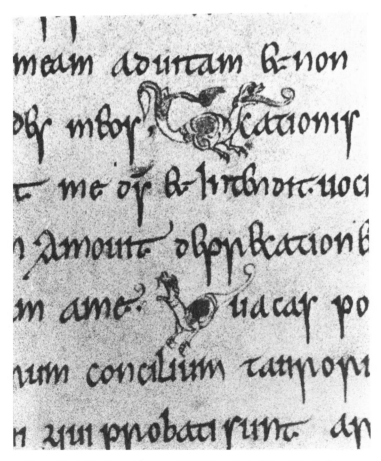

*Fig. 14 Cambridge, University Library, MS Li.I.10 (Book of Cerne), detail of text*

symbols of the Evangelists, each with wings, now six, now four, now two; here the eagle, there the calf, here the man and there the lion, and other forms almost infinite. Look at them superficially with the ordinary casual glance, and you would think it is an erasure, and not tracery. Fine craftsmanship is all about you, but you might not notice it. Look more keenly at it and you will penetrate to the very shrine of art. You will make out intricacies, so delicate and subtle, so exact and compact, so full of knots and links, with colours so fresh and vivid, that you might say that all this was the work of an angel, and not of a man. For my part, the oftener I see the book, and the more carefully I study it, the more I am lost in ever fresh amazement, and I see more and more wonders in the book.

---

40. J. O'Meara, 'Giraldus Cambrensis, In Topographia Hibernie', *P.R.I.A.*, 1949 (C), pp. 113 ff. The translation quoted here is that of Dr Alton in *E.Q.C. Cenan.*, p. 15.

*Fig. 16 Above: Vatican Library, MS Barberini Lat. 570, canon-table. Below: Maeseyck,
Church of St Catherine, fragments of Gospel-book, canon-table*

*Fig. 17 Book of Kells, Symbols of the Evangelists (f.1r)*

## Relation between the text and decoration

Before we examine its various elements in detail, it will be useful to go through the Book to see how this decoration which so staggered Giraldus Cambrensis is distributed and how it is related to the text it accompanies and illustrates.

PRELIMINARIES: f. 1r  As has been noted, the Book now starts incongruously with a composite page (pl. 1) containing on the left the end of a list of Hebrew names and on the right the four symbols of the Evangelists. The page itself and its two sections are surrounded by an elaborate frame and however difficult it is to judge its purpose now that the preceding folios have vanished, it appears as a sort of preface to the canon-tables which are displayed on the next pages and where the symbols of the Evangelists play such an essential part – 'the harmony of the four Evangelists' as Giraldus describes it. The iconography of these symbols will be studied later. Suffice here to note that on *f.* 1r they are presented in a most disconcerting way. The page has really to be turned sideways in order to see them properly. Then, from left to right they appear as Luke and John, Mark and Matthew (fig. 17). One is tempted to read from the right, but even thus the list remains odd: Matthew and Mark, John and Luke.[41] It is worth noting also that the three animal symbols are partly anthropomorphic, having human arms and hands though the rest of their bodies is completely animal.

PRELIMINARIES: THE CANON-TABLES  The canon-tables (pls. 2–9) consist of parallel lists of numbers of Eusebian sections where the same episode of the life of Christ is related in several of the Gospels. As we have seen, the sections have not been indicated in the margin of the text, so that we have here, in fact, not a serviceable tabulating device, but the occasion for a lyrical outburst on the part of the illuminators. Giraldus is certainly right in his insistence on the importance of the symbols right through the Book and one may assume that this was pointed out to him by somebody who had a long acquaintance with the manuscript. The unity and correspondence of the four texts relating to the life and teaching of Christ

is the kernel of all the decoration, which is in accord with the reluctance to break up the sacred text by the insertion of preliminaries before each of the Gospels.

As far as we know, Insular tradition did not compel the painters to use such a sumptuous introduction. Several of the Insular Gospel-books have lost their preliminaries (Lichfield, Durham A. II. 17, Rawlinson G. 167). Of the more complete ones, however, the Book of Durrow and the Echternach Gospels have their lists framed simply by ornamental bands. In the Trier and Maihingen Gospels, the canons, it is true, are under arcades, but these are of such pure Mediterranean style that one may wonder if they are not insertions or a very faithful copy. Not until we come to the Lindisfarne Gospels do we find an example of architectural framing of the canon-tables translated into an Insular idiom. In the Book of Kells, not only are the lists framed by arcades but they are usually topped by the symbol of the relevant Evangelist. To accommodate the Eusebian lists under arcades may seem at first sight a very attractive scheme, but in fact, it is highly unpractical owing to the changing numbers of entries to be compared and the variable length of the lists. It is generally accepted that a minimum of twelve pages is necessary to accommodate the lists without too many difficulties. It is possible that twelve pages were originally earmarked for the displaying of the canons in the Book of Kells, but the last two pages remained blank and, as we shall see, all sorts of catastrophes occurred in compressing the text within ten pages. Moreover, the presence of the symbols of the Evangelists above the lists is another source of worry, constantly raising the problem of making them correspond to the lists below. These symbols above canon-tables are not of very common occurrence, possibly on account of the difficulties in handling them. Among Insular manuscripts they occur, in very imperfect form, in the Maeseyck manuscript and the Barberini Gospel-book (fig. 16). It is not known where that type of canons arose. It is often assumed to be of Byzantine origin, but no Byzantine example has survived. It is found also in some Carolingian manuscripts and in a group of Spanish manuscripts somewhat later, though the link between these various series remains obscure.[42]

The canons start immediately on the verso of *f.* 1r (pl. 2)

---

41. Peter Meyer has given an accurate drawing of the symbols (*E.Q.C. Cenan.*, text vol., fig. 13), but on such a small scale that nobody seems to have noticed it. McGurk gives: man, eagle, lion, calf; and so does Werner. The order in which the symbols are presented is only unusual up to a point. There are cases when the four 'beasts' are disposed around a cross or a

figure of Christ thus:

| Homo | Aquila |
|------|--------|
| Leo  | Vitulus |

This happens on the Jouarre sarcophagus and in the Book of Durrow. The two small frames on *f.* 1r would then correspond to the two beasts on the left, then the two beasts on the right.

42. See Friend, *Canon Tables*; Henry, *Irish Art II*, pp. 84 ff.

*Fig. 18 Durham Cathedral Library, MS A.II.17, Crucifixion*

Fig. 19 Turin, University Library, MS O.IV.20, Ascension

169

*Fig. 20 Turin, University Library, MS O.IV.20, Last Judgment, details*

*Fig. 21 St Gall, Cathedral Library, MS 51, Last Judgment, detail*

and continue in a series of pairs of arcades up to *f*. 5r (pl. 9), which means eight arcades altogether.

The first pair (*ff*. 1v–2r: pls. 2–3) is meant for the first canon which contains references to passages common to all four Gospels. The arcades, in consequence, have five columns each, framing four lists. The columns have semi-circular bases and square capitals from which spring a series of small arcades. Between these and a larger arch is framed on each page an irregularly shaped tympanum with symbols of the four Evangelists, this time in their normal order, each one being more or less above the list of references from his Gospel and acting as a sort of title to it. Great effort has been devoted to varying not only their appearance but their pose. On the left hand page, the lion and calf face each other so that there is an ascending motion towards the winged figure which appears at the top of the page above the frame. On the right, there is no such figure and the symbols face each other two by two, the centre of the composition being marked by the interlaced wing patterns of the lion and calf.

Though the lay-out of the page embodies a memory of the late Antique canon-tables, only the structure of the architectural elements remains, each of them being invaded by a compact wealth of ornament from the usual Insular repertoire.

The two tables on *ff*. 2v and 3r (pls. 4–5) have a deceptively symmetrical appearance. They seem to have been designed to frame two lists on each side, those of the second canon with references to Matthew, Mark and Luke. But this canon is very long and the spaces between the columns have been fitted with double lists, those on the left divided by additional thin columns, while on the right only the bases of these columns have been drawn, the columns being omitted. The two pages have figures appearing at the top as on *f*. 1v, that on the left having a halo with three crosses. As the lists are of passages which occur in only three of the Gospels, there are three symbols in each tympanum (Matthew, Mark, Luke: pl. 101, bottom). The reappearance of a figure which seems to symbolize Matthew in one of the discs on the right is unaccountable.

The third pair of pages (*ff*. 3v–4r: pls. 6–7) shows a change in the location of the symbols which ought to have been thoroughly effective: each of them is framed in one of the small arcades so as to be exactly above the relevant list. Unfortunately this is exactly where things went wrong and the new arrangement's clearest result was to emphasize the error. On the left hand page, quite correctly, the end of the second canon has been displayed. The right had been prepared for the third canon (Matthew, Luke, John) and has its symbols (pl. 103, top). But for some unfathomable reason the lists of that third canon have been written clumsily around the bases of the arcades on the left (*f*. 3v: pl. 6). The page which had been prepared for it on the right (*f*. 4r: pl. 7) received instead the lists of the fourth canon (Matthew, Mark, John). The very equivocal appearance of the symbol in the middle arch on each side – neither calf nor lion – did certainly lend itself to the transformation. But for the sake of clarity the names of the relevant Evangelists were written on the left under the symbols and on the right above them. As in the first pair of arcades there is only one figure appearing above the frame, this time on the right, as if the six pages were conceived as a single unit with a symmetrical arrangement of these figures.

*Ff*. 4v–5r (pls. 8–9) are disconcerting: the two pages are very clearly composed to match each other, with circular bases and square capitals and a new arrangement of the small arches which are being bitten into by dragon heads. For the columns the ornaments are the same: birds, spirals and interlace, and the same fine interlace covers the arches on both sides. All this correspondence is however only in the outline drawing; the blunt colours of the left hand page have nothing in common with the subtle harmonies on the right. And in the upper part of each composition, the treatment is completely different. As if still shaken by the confusions which had occurred on the previous page, the painter of *f*. 4v has refrained from the use of symbols altogether. Instead, for this display of the lists of the fifth canon (Matthew, Luke), the names of the Evangelists are written above the frame. The tympanum and spandrels in fact seem hardly finished and may have been filled in later, judging from the odd appearance of the paint. The small arcades are filled by outsize birds whose heads nearly disappear in the complicated interlacing of their necks.

The upper part of the right hand page, *f*. 5r (pl. 9) stands in complete contrast to this. It is by far one of the most impressive compositions in the whole Book. The perfect balance of the panels of interlaced figures, human and animal, some of them with their feet casually encroaching on the frame, has a delicacy which leaves the monotonous birds of the left hand page far behind. The symbols reappear. As the lists are from two Gospels only and, each being very short, change constantly, the symbols could not be put in the small arches. But all four of them are shown: Matthew and John (pl. 102, top right) facing each other in unframed spandrels, Mark and Luke drawn in bold curves and outlined on a sky of deep purple sprayed with dots (pl. 101, top). The feeling that a different hand, and a much more masterly one, is at work above the level of the capitals is unavoidable. The bare arm of the symbol of Matthew and the human hand in that of John recall the iconography of *f*. 1r, though the incisive quality of the drawing is quite different.

There remain finally the ninth and tenth canons, made up of a series of short lists some of which are not even comparisons. Here, as in several other books, the system of arcades is abandoned and simple colour bands replace them (*ff*. 5v and 6r).[43] After these ten pages full of compressions and apparently dominated by the fear of not fitting the superabundant matter into the space available, come, unaccountably, two blank pages (*ff*. 6v and 7r), so that in fact the scribes had the necessary twelve pages at their disposal.[44] Incompetence in planning, or perhaps change of leadership, seems to have caused havoc.

---

43. The same thing happens at this point in other Insular manuscripts (P. McGurk, 'Two notes on the Book of Kells and its relation to other insular Gospel-Books', *Scriptorium*, 1955, pp. 105 ff.). These colour bands are very similar to those used for the canon-tables in the Echternach Gospels.

44. The reverse of the Virgin and Child miniature on *f*. 7v (pl. 10) may have been intended to remain blank; but there would still have been eleven pages available.

PRELIMINARIES: BREVES CAUSAE AND ARGUMENTA Of this part of the Book we have seen the somewhat incoherent disposition, inherited from the Book of Durrow or its exemplar. If now we turn to the decoration, we are faced, except at the very end, with a fairly consistent treatment.

The prefaces are heralded by a pair of decorated pages facing each other, such as we shall find at the opening of some of the Gospels (ff. 7v–8r): on the right are the fantastically elaborated first lines of the *Breves causae* of Matthew, starting with *Nativitas XPI in Bethlem Iudeae*; opposite, on the left, are the Virgin and Child surrounded by angels, an icon and not the Nativity scene or an Adoration of the Magi which would have been justified by the continuation of the text (*Magi munera offerunt*). The text page is of a lovely intricacy, with a change in the treatment of the letters from line to line, the first line being partly written in elongated and curved animal letters. The text on the following pages has a great wealth of small unelaborated initials surrounded by dots and tiny sprays of foliage.

At first it may have been intended to start each chapter at the top of a page. This is the case with the *Argumentum* of Matthew (f. 12r: pl. 12, top), introduced by a massive M partly hiding a figure with two stems of foliage and followed by a jumble of angular-shaped letters. But from the *Breves causae* of Mark (f. 13r) onwards a continuous arrangement of the text prevails, with a series of chapter-headings that are very elaborate and minute in treatment (pls. 12, below, ff.), remarkably similar to those at the beginning of the Gospel extracts in the Prayer-book of Cerne. They have some strange aspects: while the beginning of the *Breves causae* of Mark does not include any allusion to the symbol of the Evangelist, there are several little lions included in the cartouche preceding his

*Argumentum* (pl. 13, above). However, there are more lions and nothing suggesting a calf at the beginning of the *Breves causae* of Luke (pl. 14, below). A complete change comes with the *Breves causae* of John, which are only introduced by a thin initial I made of the erect figure of a cat without the usual cartouche of ornamental letters (pl. 17).

THE GOSPELS: GENERAL PLAN OF DECORATION It is tempting to try and reconstruct what was originally the general plan of decoration for the Gospels – assuming, of course, that the chief scribe or painter had a general plan in mind. What we have seen so far gives such an odd impression of an empirical approach and of constant readjustments that one may wonder whether it was so. However, we have for two of the Gospels a consistent scheme of decoration which allows us to assume that it was followed originally right through.

As was usual everywhere, the chief decorative effort centred on the beginnings of the Gospels. It can be summed up thus:

MATTHEW    page with four symbols (f. 27v: pl. 20)
       portrait of the Evangelist (f. 28v: pl. 22)
       *Liber*, Introductory page with the first few words of the Gospel (f. 29r: pl. 23)
MARK    page with four symbols (f. 129v: pl. 50)
       *Initium*, Introductory page (f. 130r: pl. 51)
LUKE    *Quoniam*, Introductory page (f. 188r: pl. 61)
JOHN    page with four symbols (f. 290v: pl. 92)
       portrait of the Evangelist (f. 291v: pl. 94)
       *In principio*, Introductory page (f. 292r: pl. 95)

This seems to give a standard arrangement: page of symbols – portrait – Introductory page. It might mean that we

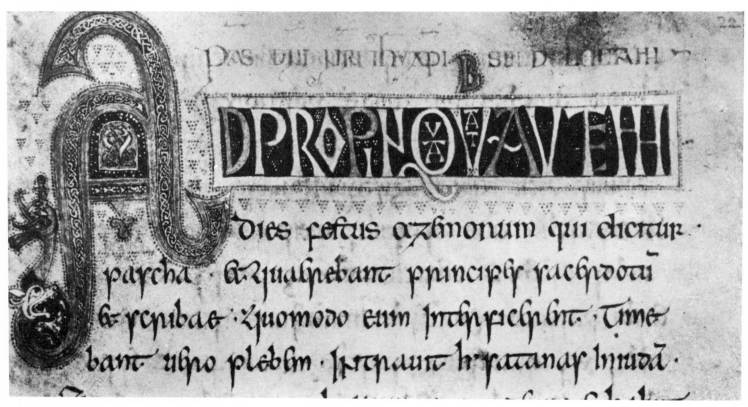

Fig. 22 Cambridge, University Library, MS Li.I.10 (Book of Cerne), beginning of the
Passion according to St John

have lost one page of symbols, that of Luke, and two portraits, those of Mark and Luke.[45]

In addition to this, the genealogy of Matthew is dealt with, as in several Insular manuscripts and indeed some Continental ones, as if it was a separate book, the text immediately following Matthew I, 18 being given a treatment similar to that of the beginning of a Gospel: portrait of Christ, carpet-page, Introductory page (*XPI autem generatio*; pls. 26, 27, 29). This tendency to separate the genealogy from the rest of the text is even more marked in late Irish manuscripts, so much so that in one of them, in the twelfth century, completely irrelevant texts are inserted between the two.[46]

Then the three synoptic Gospels have, or had, or were to have, illustrated pages dealing with some important event described in the text. In Matthew, there is the Arrest of Christ, which marks the beginning of the Passion. It is accompanied on its verso by a page of decorated text, *Tunc dicit* (ff. 114r and v: pls. 45, 46). A blank page in the same Gospel, on *f.* 123v, was no doubt reserved for a Crucifixion. The preceding page, *f.* 123r, contains only fifteen lines instead of the usual seventeen, and they are deliberately spaced to end with the text of the Titulum, while the blank page is faced with a page of ornamented text: *Tunc crucifixerant XPI cum eo duos latrones* (*f.* 124r: pl. 47).

The Gospel of St Mark has only two such pages, both rather disconcerting. One of them is a page of ornamental text, *Erat autem hora tercia* (*f.* 183r: pls. 55 and 126), with an angel in a sitting position – though with nothing to sit on – holding a book. This has an extremely odd arrangement of frame, with the bust of a figure appearing on the right, while his feet appear below the frame on the left. Was this also meant to accompany a Crucifixion, as the text would imply, or a Resurrection, as the attitude of the angel may suggest, or is it itself a representation of the Resurrection, with the partly hidden figure standing for Christ?

The last page of Mark (*f.* 187v: pl. 58) has given rise to speculation. Its saltire-shaped division may suggest a comparison with the arrangement of the four-symbols page of John. It has been surmised that it was meant originally to be part of the ornamented pages at the beginning of Luke. However, it bears the text relating to the Ascension at the end of Mark and an inscription which reaches across the page describes the winged figure on the left as *angelus dn̄i*. The symbol of St Mark on the right seems more a sort of conclusion to the Gospel than an element of an unfinished symbols page. It may be that the page was meant to bear a picture of the Ascension, such as is found in the Turin Gospels, where the *angelus Domini* would have his normal place and that this scheme was forestalled by an unforeseen overflow of the text. There would have been room in the upper triangle for a figure of Christ and in the lower triangle for the Apostles. Such an upset as the abandonment of this original scheme because of a miscalculation of the scribe would be perfectly in keeping with what we have seen in the canon-tables. It is worth noting that the two large beasts whose legs form the X division of the page have a very close parallel in a manuscript now in the Cathedral Treasury at Essen which probably comes from Corbie and is a late example of those northern French manuscripts which occasionally have such remarkable kinship with the Book of Kells.

In the Gospel of St Luke we find another surviving illustration, that of the Temptation of Christ on the Temple (*f.* 202v: pl. 68) facing a page of ornamental text. As in the case of the Arrest, it acts as an introduction to a whole section of the sacred text, the public life of Christ. But while the picture of the Arrest did not fit exactly with the very words describing the event, here the ornamented text on the opposite page, *Jesus autem plenus S.S.*, is exactly the beginning of the story of the Temptation. On *f.* 285r (pl. 89), another page of ornamented text, *Una autem sabbati valde de lu* . . ., marks the beginning of the story of the Resurrection. It is not likely to have faced an illustration, as that would have had some text on the back and no text is missing. Around the ornamental text are disposed four winged figures. Finally, one may wonder if a blank page at the end of the Gospel (*f.* 289v) was meant for an illustration.[47] The writing on *f.* 289r is slightly compressed as if in an effort not to encroach on it. The text of the end of the Gospel relates to the Ascension, which would presumably have been the subject of the illustration, unless the painter, thinking in more general terms, had perhaps chosen to represent the Last Judgment.

The Gospel of St John as it stands now has no illustration, but as the whole of the Passion narrative is missing, there may well have been one or two. The surviving illustrations in Matthew and Luke, the Arrest and the Temptation (pls. 45, 68), appear to act as introductions to large sections of their respective Gospels. We have suggested the possibility that two pictures of the Crucifixion and two of the Ascension were originally planned; it is not absolutely impossible that this very redundancy was the reason why some of the pictures were not executed.

This rapid review of the illustrated pages, which will be complemented later by a detailed study of their iconography, has revealed no very definite scheme in the choice and distribution of the subjects. As each of them seems to have been accompanied by a page of ornamented text, it is unwise to assume that there were originally more illustrations than those which have been mentioned and that they were later lost.

The pages of ornamental text deserve study. They are of two types: either they are meant to accompany an illustration, as do *ff.* 114v, 124r and 202v for the Arrest, the Crucifixion and the Temptation respectively (pls. 46, 47, 68), or they stand by themselves, being in fact semi-illustrations, as they incorporate figures relevant to that part of the Gospel. This is the case for the *Erat autem* (*f.* 183r: pl. 55) and the *Una autem* (*f.* 285r: pl. 89). The two figured pages in the Turin manuscript present, up to a point, a parallel to these two types of illustrations: the Last Judgment (fig. 20) is a pictorial composition filling the page completely, while in the Ascension page (fig. 19) text and figures are constantly mixed, though

45. These could be the three pages missing from Ussher's count between *f.* 99 (*recte* 100) and *f.* 196 (*recte* 197) – see above, n. 23 – assuming that the folio of text missing after *f.* 177 was already lost when Ussher made his count (see p. 150). The missing charters could have been written on their blank reverse (see n. 5).

46. F. Henry and G. L. Marsh-Micheli, 'A century of Irish Illumination (1070–1170)', *P.R.I.A.*, 1962 (C), pp. 101 ff. (see pp. 148 and 152).

47. *F.* 289 is thinner than the pages generally used for full-page illustrations, but it would hardly have been left blank without a purpose.

Fig. 23 Book of Kells, initial (f. 96r)

the text is in ordinary majuscules and not in ornamented letters.

Finally, it is important to note that originally the two pages (symbols page and portrait) at the beginning of each Gospel and the two pages (portrait and carpet-page) before Matthew I, 18 can be assumed to have been planned with blank reverses. It was only through mishandling of the text that some of them were used for writing. On the other hand, Introductory pages (including the Chi-Rho) and illustrations are part and parcel of the text and have no such blank reverses, thus avoiding unseemly breaks in the narrative.

## Ornaments in the text

Leaving aside the spectacular full-page illuminations, it will now be useful, in order to form a general impression of the Book, to turn the pages of the Gospel texts one by one so as to get some idea of their embellishments.

GOSPEL OF ST MATTHEW After the symbols page, portrait and Introductory page comes the genealogy (ff. 29v–31v: pls. 24–25). It was meant to be lavishly framed, but the decoration was never finished and is in most places no more than a delicate drawing with here and there some indications of colour. Owing to the presence of the frame, there are only fourteen lines on f. 29v. Then the three following pages are given no more than thirteen lines, a device which spares exactly the three lines occupying the verso of f. 31 and enables the painter to treat the three pages after the genealogy (portrait of Christ, carpet-page, Monogram page) like the beginning of a Gospel, starting with a blank recto.

After the large Monogram page (f. 34r: pl. 29) and up to f. 40v (pl. 30) the initials are fairly evenly spread out and of comparatively small size. However, they are much more elaborate and diversified than the monotonous letters filled with colour in the preliminaries. Many of them correspond with

beginnings of the un-numbered Eusebian sections. The sprays of foliage are replaced here by little rosettes often arranged in rows.

On f. 40v (pl. 30), the first eight Beatitudes are emphasized by a continuous vertical band of purple on which the Bs are outlined. They are made of four human and four animal figures twisted to the shapes of the letters. A little further on, the *Pater noster* (f. 45: pl. 31) starts rather clumsily at the bottom of a page with an over-large animal initial which encroaches deeply on the lower margin.

The text goes on, with a fairly consistent amount of initials and many little animals filling gaps or indicating 'turns'. Their quality varies, however. At first, they belong to a sort of decorative routine. Then much more imaginative creations appear, usually several on the same page or on consecutive pages. Very few seem to have a close connection with the meaning of the corresponding text. However, at the parable of the sower – *Vos autem audite parabulam seminantis* (Matt. XIII, 18) the cock and hens which walk so firmly over the letters (f. 67r: pl. 120) must surely illustrate the birds which eat the seed, and the crouching figure inside the capital V (really U) may well be meant for *malignus* who interferes with the good seed. On f. 96r, when the Pharisees are reported to be plotting *ut caperent eum in sermone* (Matt. XIII, 15), one might be tempted to think that the figure in the initial, twisted and sinister, represents the Pharisee and that the gorgeous bird it is catching in both hands may represent Christ (fig. 23). We shall examine such problems of interpretation later, but it is useful also to indicate them here. Omissions are just as striking: why, for example, is the parable of the workmen in the vineyard completely devoid of vine sprays when they are so common in some parts of the Book? And was there not a good chance of painting a fish, instead of the irrelevant cat indicating an added letter, at the story of the tribute money (f. 81r; Matt. XVII, 24 ff.)? Unaccountably, such a fish appears on f. 84v where nothing seems to warrant its presence.

The Passion, which opens with the illustration of the Arrest and was meant to have a representation of the Crucifixion, shows an even greater wealth and resourcefulness in the treatment of the initials. The proportion of those made of elongated animals is very high and a sort of anguished feeling grows out of their constant agitation. This is perhaps the real way in which they relate to the text, as music does to the words of a song, and in looking for absolutely literal illustrations we are often wasting our time and misunderstanding the mood of the painter.

An irregularity in the number of lines of some of the pages is also part of this subtle orchestration. As we have seen, there are only fifteen lines on the page which would have preceded the Crucifixion (f. 123r). Then there are only twelve on the reverse of the page which bears the ornamented *Tunc crucifixerant* (f. 124r: pl. 47). The text on that page consists of the commentaries and sarcasms of the Jews at the Crucifixion (Matt. XXVII, 39 ff.). There may have been some intention of isolating it. But it is possible also that the two short pages are meant to balance each other. On f. 127r again there are only twelve lines. This has been done, obviously, to allow the *Vespere autem* which, on the reverse, starts the story of the Resurrection, to be at the top of a page (pl. 48). Unfortunately, all this spacing out meant an excess of twelve lines over what had no doubt been foreseen for the text of Matthew, and as a consequence the end of that text is clumsily brought over to the reverse of the first decorated page of Mark (f. 129r) where it ends with an *explicit* but no *incipit*.

GOSPEL OF ST MARK The initials in the second Gospel are at first of an extremely simple type and in fact present a good parallel in their timid demeanour with those in the first pages of the text proper of Matthew. Little rosettes are again a very prominent feature. But occasionally sprays of foliage are used also (f. 133r). Here the most striking element of each initial is the thick black line which gives it its general shape. It is not until f. 166v that a ribbon-animal initial appears, then again on ff. 169r, 173v, 174r. Up to that point the 'turns' are mostly of a very sober type and only a few animals walk in the blank spaces. Again, as in St Matthew's Gospel, it is when we reach the Passion that the painter seems to give a freer rein to his imagination. The two pages dealing with the Crucifixion (ff. 183v and 184r: pls. 56, 57) are marked by a series of initials of incredible vehemence. The following pages are calmer in appearance, but still lavishly decorated. On f. 185v there is a definite alternation of black line letters and ribbon-animal ones, a system which became common in later Irish manuscripts such as the Southampton Psalter and some of the late eleventh-twelfth century books.

GOSPEL OF ST LUKE After the short prologue of this Gospel, a large capital marks the beginning of the Childhood story, and there the lion—possibly the Lion of Judah – holding a bough in its mouth, and the fishes, symbols of Christ, have fairly obvious meanings. But after this the utmost severity reigns, broken only for the beginning of the Magnificat and the Canticle of Zacharias. Afterwards, miserable little ornamented letters appear here and there. But decoration only comes into its own with the genealogy (ff. 200r–202r: pls. 63–67). A system similar to that used in the Beatitudes in Matthew obtains here: the *Qui* which begin each line are linked together by the continuous ornament formed by their first letters. These

letters have zoomorphic endings which fight with a series of birds and animals. Only the top letter of f. 200r (pl. 63) is made of a human figure, very tall and elongated. On the third page (f. 201r: pl. 65), the system changes and each letter is formed by a drawn out and twisted animal body. On f. 201v (pl. 66) the chain is partly made of real letters, except in the upper part where five human figures are elaborately interlaced (pl. 117). The genealogy ends with a magnificent tail-piece of birds and foliage (pl. 109).

After this brilliant episode, the painter follows a kind of middle course in his decorative style, without, however, reverting to the starkness of the first pages. The Beatitudes are marked by a chain of initials, as in Matthew, though they are more lightly presented.

Occasionally, as on ff. 212v–213r, a pair of pages is earmarked for an especially brilliant decoration, though nothing in the text seems to warrant that choice. On f. 218v (pl. 72), however, a discreet arrangement of crosses and foliage draws attention to the story of Mary Magdalene. Similarly, the parable of the Prodigal Son (Luke XV, 11) is marked by a fantastically elaborate initial (f. 250v). Though the *Pater* on f. 234v starts with a large P, it is no more prominently decorated than in the Gospel of St Matthew.

It is obvious that, as the painter progresses in his text, he warms up to his work and lets himself go more and more. Though some of the very few undecorated pages in the Book are found there, they alternate with most fanciful pages where animals, birds and little human figures vie with each other, encroach on each other's space, accompanying the text with a brilliant embroidery.

*Fig. 24 Dublin, Trinity College Library, MS 57 (Book of Durrow), beginning of St Mark's Gospel*

*Fig. 25 Paris, National Library, MS Lat. 9389 (Echternach Gospels), beginning of St Luke's Gospel*

The two pages of the Crucifixion narrative are not, in Luke, marked by any special elaboration. The *Una autem* page of the Resurrection is really incorporated in the text and the last few pages revert to the sobriety of the early part of the Gospel.

After the blank page (*f.* 289v) which ends the Gospel and was probably earmarked for an illustration, there is, on the reverse of the four-symbols page of John (*f.* 290r) a magnificently written *explicit-incipit* whose calligraphy shields an incoherent wording.

GOSPEL OF ST JOHN What is left of the Gospel of St John is hardly remarkable for the wealth of its decoration, but one must keep in mind the fact that in the other Gospels the Passion is the part which is most elaborately treated, and here the whole text of the Passion is missing.

The initials, right through, are very simple, mostly drawn in black lines but with a tendency to end the letters with the flourish of a little head. One pair of pages (*ff.* 309v: pl. 98–

*f.* 310r), that dealing with the Bread of Life (John VI, 43–57), is much more brilliantly decorated. The Good Shepherd (John X, 1 ff.; *f.* 323r) and the resurrection of Lazarus (John XI, 1–44; *ff.* 325r–327v) both have a continuous if rather uninspired stream of initials and small animals, and there is quite an exuberant bird for the entry into Jerusalem (*f.* 329v).

The last folio, very rubbed, ends with John XVII, 13, that is to say a little before the conclusion of the speech of Christ at the Last Supper (John XVIII is the beginning of the Passion). This makes it futile to try to estimate the quality of the decoration of the Gospel as it once was.[48]

---

48. As the surviving part of the Gospel of St John is written in pages of eighteen lines, the writing itself is here more crowded than in the other Gospels and in consequence there is less possibility for an exuberant decoration. But we do not know whether the Passion was written in the same way.

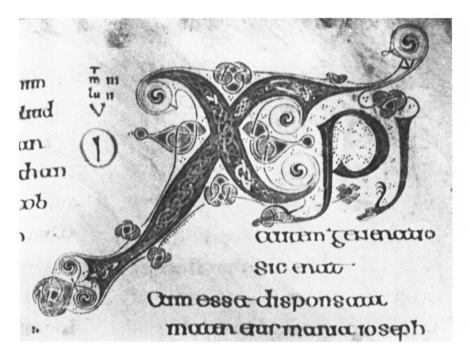

*Fig. 26 Left : Schloss Harburg, 'Maihingen Gospels', Chi-Rho.*
*Below : Lichfield, Cathedral, Lichfield Gospels, Chi-Rho*

*Fig. 27 St Gall, Cathedral Library, MS 51, Chi-Rho*

XPI

AU TEM
SIC ERAT CUM
DONSATAMA
MARIA IOSEph
QUAM CONUE
INUENTA
INUTERO
DESpu
Ioseph AU
CUM ESSET b

CENERATIO
ESSET DIS
TER EIUS
ANTE
NIRENT
EST
BENS

hA
SCO
TAM CUR
CNO TUS

*Fig. 28 Vatican Library, MS Barberini Lat. 570, Chi-Rho*

179

## Composition of full-page decorated pages

The presentation of the large decorated pages is very interesting. One of its outstanding characteristics is the fact that whatever the 'picture' it is generally presented within a frame or at least a partial frame. This is manifest even in the canon-tables where, with one exception only (*f.* 5r: pl. 9) the arches are squared up with spandrels.

This frame may be continuous, like an ordinary picture frame, or it may be interrupted in one or several places. The little panels containing human busts which are found on two pages (*ff.* 7v, 124r; pls. 10, 47) are hardly relevant as they are either superimposed on or inserted in recesses of the frame, which in fact remains continuous. But there are other cases where the frame develops an animal's head at one end confronting his tail across a slight gap (*ff.* 1r, 124r, etc.: pls. 1, 47).

The pages of ornamental text, Monogram, *Nativitas* and Introductory pages of the Gospels, have partial frames, as the first letters are enlarged to reach to the top and bottom of the available space and the frame serves only to complete them on the right. The result is an extraordinary richness of pattern, the irregular outline of the letters compensating for the rigidity of the frame. It might at first appear that the letters were origin-ally enclosed in a frame and broke through only in a late phase of gigantism. In fact, the contrary is true. If one follows the evolution of the Monogram page in various manuscripts, this will appear clearly: in the Book of Durrow, the Maihingen (fig. 26) and Echternach Gospels, the Chi-Rho is no more than some enlarged letters treated as ornament in a page of ordinary writing. In the Lichfield and St Gall Gospels, extraordinarily similar to each other at this point (figs. 26, 27), the frame exists on the right and at the bottom of the page, but there are three lines of text. So also in the Lindisfarne Gospels, where the letters have kept their quality of script. In the Book of Kells, a fluid mass of ornament covers the whole page, connecting the Chi-Rho with the frame and leaving room for only two words in ordinary script. So it looks as if the frames were introduced as a natural curb to the exuberance of pattern when the letters grew outsize.

The same thing applies to the Introductory pages: the Book of Durrow has enlarged ornamental letters only, without a frame (fig. 24). In Durham MS A. II. 17 and MS 197 in Corpus Christi College, Cambridge, the letters reach to the bottom of the page, but there is no frame. The Leningrad Gospels, giving a similar impression at first sight, have in fact a frame of dotted lines imitating filigree work. In the Lichfield

*Fig. 29 Milan, Ambrosian Library, MS D.23.sup. (Chronicle of Orosius; from Bobbio),*
*opening pages*

Fig. 30 Turin, University Library, MS O.IV.20, page of ornaments

181

(fig. 26) and Lindisfarne Gospels there are thin frames, but several lines of decorative text follow the first enlarged letter. Here the notion of text still exists and is clearly stressed. In the Book of Kells two or three words, sometimes one only (*Quoniam*), are hidden in the fantastic display of ornament. Instead of displaying a sentence meant to be read these pages have become *objets d'art*. They present a sort of rebus, as for example the *Initium* of St Mark's Gospel (*f*. 130r: pl. 51), and ordinary writing becomes an anticlimax when we turn the page.

Another type of ornamental page which is usually called a 'carpet-page' early assumed an important place in Insular manuscripts. It is a page of pure ornament which in most cases is completely reversible and can be viewed either way up without upsetting the pattern. This has almost probably an Oriental and more specifically a Coptic origin. It is found already in an early Irish manuscript from Bobbio, the Orosius in the Ambrosian Library, probably its first occurrence in Insular art (fig. 29). It occupies a place of great importance in the Book of Durrow and the Lindisfarne Gospels. But it may be that the carpet-page lost favour after a time. The fact that there is only one in the Lichfield Gospels is not significant, as the book is incomplete. But the Maihingen and St Gall

Gospels also have no more than one; and so with the Book of Kells, that tremendous double cross with circular ends, the 'page of the eight circles' which may originally have faced the Chi-Rho, though it is now bound so as to face the portrait of Christ (*f*. 331; pl. 27).

In all these pages, the density of the ornament is disciplined and distributed by means of the wide bands of bright colour, blue, purple, yellow, etc., which draw across the page regular, almost geometric patterns. They are often the first element to be registered clearly by the eye when confronted with that maze of ornament. They play the same role as the frames which enclose and limit various designs in Irish or Scottish metalwork. In fact the Tara brooch has large bands of inset tablets of amber which are closely parallel in colour effect to the yellow angular ribbons which run across the Introductory pages of the book.[49] In the ornamental text pages there is, in addition, an energetic way of reinforcing the outline of the first large letters by stressing it with a strong black line. This again is not an invention of the Kells painters. The same feature is found in the Durham MS A. II. 17, the Lindisfarne Gospels and some pages of the Lichfield Gospels (fig. 26). But in the Book of Kells it is a regular and powerfully handled means of constructing a decorative page.

*Fig. 31 Vatican Library, MS Barberini Lat. 570,*
*detail of Chi-Rho page*

49. Henry, *Irish Art I*, pls. 40–41.

# ICONOGRAPHY

The figurative elements in the Book of Kells consist of four full-page figures (three portraits and the Virgin and Child), two illustrations (the Arrest of Christ and the Temptation), various representations of the symbols of the Evangelists, several groups of four angels, various figures, some winged, several of them holding books, and figures included in the Introductory pages of Matthew, Mark and John. If some of these are not easy of interpretation, at least it is clear that they are intended to have a meaning. After that we pass to that hazy borderland between ornament and illustration which gives the Book its mysterious depth, where one fears to interpret too much and lend an esoteric meaning to what is simply intended as a beautiful play of lines, while a few significant details seem to excuse bold speculation. However, a reluctance to venture upon too much interpretation will explain why a few details which might have been dealt with here appear in the chapter on ornament.

## The portraits

There are three full-page figures in the Book which are obviously meant as portraits, one of Matthew, one of John, and one probably of Christ; and it is more than likely that there were also portraits of Mark and Luke.

Portraits of the Evangelists are no novelty in Insular manuscripts and indeed they appear also in many other Gospel-books of the time, whether Oriental, Italian or Carolingian, wherever the symbols of the Evangelists do not replace them. Some show the Evangelists nearly in profile and writing. This is the attitude of Ezra in the Codex Amiatinus, of most of the Evangelists in the Lindisfarne Gospels and the Maeseyck manuscript and of the St Matthew in St Gall MS 1395 (figs. 11, 39). Except for the last, these pictures are all marked by a very pronounced Greek or Italian influence.[50] In many other cases the Evangelists are shown full face, sitting or sometimes standing, occasionally holding a pen or some other object. This is the case with the Lichfield Evangelists (fig. 44), those in St Gall MS 51, in the Book of Dimma, the Book of Mulling, the Stowe St John and the later Book of Mac Durnan.

The Kells portraits belong to the full-face type. It is also important to note that in spite of what seems at first sight a standing position, the figures are all meant to be sitting. In fact Matthew (pl. 22) and John (pl. 94) are both shown on a large chair whose arms and back are covered with draperies.

The furniture has been so completely dissociated into fragments that the arms of Matthew's chair can only be understood by reference to St John's portrait. That both chairs are meant to have a high back covered by a drapery becomes intelligible when they are compared with similar but more coherent representations, such as the Evangelist portraits in some Carolingian manuscripts.[51] Both figures have a nimbus, that of John especially elaborate. Both Evangelists hold a book with a decorated cover, Matthew in his left hand and seemingly resting it on his lap, while John holds his aloft. But John's gesture is ambiguous, as his right hand grasps a long quill which he is preparing to dip in a small ink-horn standing on the edge of the frame near his right foot. These arrangements are unusual, as full-face Insular Evangelists generally hold their book with both hands, slightly on their left side or in front of them (St Mark in Lichfield, St Luke in St Gall MS 51, etc.).[52] St John in the Gospels of Mac Durnan also dips a pen in an ink-horn while holding a book and eraser in his left hand. There is an ink-horn in the Lichfield portrait of St Mark though it is not in use and the Evangelists in the Barberini Gospels have at their disposition various ink-pots (fig. 12).

The Kells St Matthew is accompanied by the symbols of the three other Evangelists, the calf and eagle appearing over the arms of the chair and two lion busts doing duty as the symbol of Mark as well as decorating the back of the chair. The St Mark portraits in the Book of Lichfield and the Book of Mac Durnan have chairs with such emblematic terminals. But so has the Kells Virgin (f. 7v: pl. 10), so that in this case the representation of a certain type of furniture possibly current at the time seems to be combined with a suggestion of an Evangelical symbol. The representation in some guise or other, of the four symbols on the page preceding the Gospel of St Matthew is a feature of some Insular manuscripts (St Gall 51, Book of Armagh), so that the presence of the three animal symbols around the portrait of St Matthew is only normal.

Both apostles are shown with bare feet, or more probably wearing sandals, the lines on their feet representing straps as they do in many Byzantine manuscripts. The usual medieval tradition is to show the apostles bare-footed, a sign of their poverty. But this was by no means the general rule in the earlier period we are dealing with. Sandals are common in Byzantine manuscripts and shoes appear here and there in Insular manuscripts, little low boots in the case of St Matthew in St Gall MS 1395, the Evangelists of the Book of Mulling

---

50. Even the St Gall page shows classical influence; see n. 37.
51. Friend, *Canon Tables*.

52. This is the correct way for apostles and saints to hold their books, from Bawit to Ravenna.

Fig. 32 Ravenna, Church of S. Apollinare in Classe, sarcophagus of Archbishop Theodore
(c. 460)

and the St John of the Stowe manuscript. The St Mark of the Book of Dimma seems to have slippers, but they may simply be the same type of shoe seen from above (fig. 33). So no fixed rule can be established.

The portrait of St Matthew is framed by an arch whose columns, with their circular bases and square capitals, are strangely reminiscent of the architecture of the canon-tables. By some queer whimsy, they have however been bent right and left so that the arch is supported on the side and not on the top of the capitals.

The portrait of St John is contained in an elaborate frame behind which appears a haloed figure with arms outstretched, unfortunately cut into by the early nineteenth-century binder. The figure does not actually hold up the frame, but his head, closed fist and feet emerge from it. He will be examined later, together with a series of similar figures from the canon-tables and the genealogy of St Luke.

The figure under an arch on f. 32v (pl. 26) has sometimes been thought of as the displaced portrait of another Evangelist (Mark or Luke). It is now generally accepted as representing Christ. The figure has again a deceptive standing appearance, but the arms and sides of a chair are clearly shown on both sides. The head is in full face, with golden, curly hair, blue eyes and a dark moustache and beard. He seems to be support-ing a book in his veiled left hand while holding it with his right hand, slightly to the left. The book is closed, but its side as well as cover are shown.[53] The feet are bare or more prob-ably wearing sandals. In these details the figure does not differ much from the two Evangelist portraits and, like the figure of St Matthew, it is framed by bent columns supporting an arch. The right hand is not shown blessing as is usual in depictions of Christ. The attributes which accompany the figure are the real clue to its meaning. In the semi-circular space which serves as a halo, two peacocks are shown flanking a small cross.

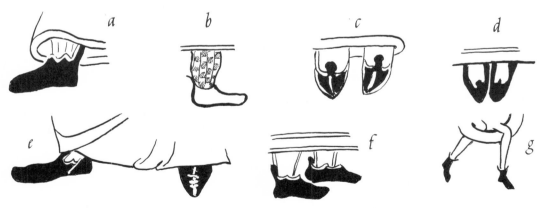

Fig. 33 Shoes: a Dublin, Trinity College Library, MS 60 (Book of Mulling); b Id. MS 57 (Book of Durrow); c London, Lambeth Palace Library, Book of Mac Durnan; d Dublin, Trinity College Library, MS 59 (Book of Dimma); e Vatican Library, MS Barberini Lat. 570; f St Gall, Cathedral Library, MS 1395; g Book of Kells, Beatitudes (f. 40v)

---

53. The difference of presentation of the book occurs also in Bawit
(Wessel, Coptic Art, pls. VII, XIV and fig. 100).

Each looks intently at a small disc stamped with a cross on his own wing and the feet of both are entangled in the foliage of vines issuing from chalice-shaped vases. Further down, below the capitals, two winged figures stand on the left, while on the right a figure with no visible wings holds a flowering bough and another has at least two pairs of wings. In spite of this unevenness of presentation, they may be meant for the four archangels who also seem to accompany the Virgin and Child and are found elsewhere in the Book.

Even though the interpretation of the figure as that of Christ is convincing it remains no less surprising because at this period one would expect to find here a *Majestas Domini,* the representation of Christ as seen in the Apocalyptic Vision, between the four 'beasts'. That it had already become well-known in the West by the time the Book of Kells was painted is shown by the sarcophagus of Agilbertus in the crypt at Jouarre (late seventh century, fig. 46), the manuscript

*Fig. 35 Moscow, Pushkin Museum, Alexandrian Chronicle, Virgin and Child*

*Fig. 36 Durham, Cathedral Museum, St Cuthbert's coffin, Virgin and Child*

from Sainte-Croix in the Poitiers Library (fig. 48), which comes from the Amiens region and dates from the early ninth century, and, nearer geographically to the Book of Kells, the late seventh- or early eighth-century wooden coffin of St Cuthbert, from Lindisfarne, now in the Cathedral Museum at Durham,[54] a page of the Codex Amiatinus,[55] and the early ninth century Cross of the Tower at Kells (fig. 72).[56] In a book where the symbols of the Evangelists are omnipresent their absence in the very place where they would be especially expected is remarkable.

## The Virgin and Child

The picture of the Virgin and Child (pl. 10) is the first of the full-page illustrations in the Book. We have seen that it pairs up with the elaborately decorated Introductory page of the *Breves causae* of Matthew which starts with *Nativitas Christi in Bethlem Iudeae*. But, as we have noticed, the picture of the Virgin is not presented as a scene of the Childhood. It is a stark, imposing and immobile icon of the Virgin enthroned holding the Child and surrounded by angels. She wears a veil closely framing her face; she is draped in a purple mantle held by a lozenge-shaped brooch and sits stiffly on a chair arranged sideways in relation to the surface of the painting. The Child, sitting in 'complementary profile', turns towards her and holds her hand.

The figure has been studied by Kitzinger, Friend and Werner, who all emphasized the fact that this is the first representation of the Virgin in a Western manuscript.[57] As far as Eastern ones are concerned, the only earlier full-page representation is found in the late sixth-century Syriac Gospels of Rabbula (fig. 34). However, though it is not a full-page illustration, it is important in this context not to overlook an earlier picture in the Alexandrian World Chronicle in the Pushkin Museum in Moscow usually dated *c.* 400 A.D.[58] There, the Child is sitting sideways and has a halo, while the Virgin is full-face, with no halo (fig. 35). Coptic manuscripts of a slightly later date than the Book of Kells supply us with very striking parallels.[59] It is necessary also to remember that there were in both East and West large icons of the Virgin and Child of which some examples have survived. The Madonnas from the Monastery of St Catherine on Mount Sinai[60] and the Churches of Santa Francesca Romana[61] and Santa Maria in Trastevere[62] in Rome support the idea of the universality of this type of painting in the early Middle Ages. One such icon had been brought from Rome to Wearmouth in the late seventh century[63] and it probably inspired the group incised on one of the ends of St Cuthbert's coffin, now at Durham

54. *Relics of St Cuthbert*, pp. 202 ff.
55. Kendrick, *Anglo-Saxon Art*, pl. XLII; *E.Q.C. Lind.*, pl. 24.
56. Henry, *Irish Art II*, pl. 74.
57. E. Kitzinger, 'The Coffin-Reliquary', *Relics of St Cuthbert*, pp. 202 ff.; Friend, *Canon Tables*; Werner, *Madonna and Child*. See also V. Lazareff, 'Studies in the Iconography of the Virgin', *Art. Bull.*, 1938, pp. 46 ff.
58. J. Strzygowski and A. Bauer, *Eine Alexandrinische Weltchronik*, Vienna, 1906.
59. H. Hyvernat, *Bibliothecae Pierpont Morgan Codices Coptici Photo-*

*graphice expressi*, Rome, 1922, XX, pl. 2 (Codex M.612, dated 893).
60. G. M. Sotirou, *Les icones du Mont Sinai*, Athens, 1956, fig. 4.
61. E. Kitzinger, 'On some Icons of the Seventh Century', *Late Classical and Medieval Studies in Honour of A. M. Friend, Jr.*, Princeton, 1955, pp. 132 ff.; P. Cellini, 'Una Madonna molto antica', *Proporzioni*, 1950, pp. 1 ff.
62. C. Bertelli, *La Madonna di Santa Maria in Trastevere*, Rome, 1961.
63. C. Plummer, *Venerabilis Baedae Opera Historica*, Oxford, 1896, I, p. 369 (*Historia Abbatum*).

Fig. 37 Iona, St Martin's Cross, detail

Fig. 38 Monasterboice, Cross of Muiredach, Adoration of the Magi, detail

(fig. 36). Inspiration from similar paintings may be assumed for carvings which can be compared with the Kells miniature, the Virgin and Child surrounded by two or four angels carved on crosses at Iona (fig. 37) and Kildalton (Islay), in the West of Scotland.[64]

Though the Virgin and Child with angels is not found on Irish crosses, the Adoration of the Magi is frequently represented. In the northern group[65] (Clones, Camus-Macosquin, etc.) the Virgin is shown full face. On the contrary, on the Cross of Muiredach at Monasterboice, a short distance from Kells, she is exactly in the pose of the Kells picture (fig. 38). The same probably applies to the Holy Family at Duleek, still in the same neighbourhood, but there, the stone is so worn that it is difficult to be certain. As the Cross of Muiredach belongs to the first years of the tenth century, this may show that the Book was already in Kells at that time.

The representation in the Book of Kells has some very remarkable features. One of them is the fact that the chair and legs of the Virgin are shown sideways while her bust and head are practically frontal. This attitude is not isolated amongst Insular miniatures. It is in fact the attitude of three of the Lindisfarne Evangelists, borrowed from Greek models. It reappears, softened and already mildly incorporated in the current of Insular figure-style, in the single surviving Evangelist of the Maeseyck manuscript (fig. 39). Later it is found again in the David playing the harp of the Cotton Psalter (Vitellius F.XI). But in the case of the Kells miniature there is the additional feature of the Child being in complementary profile to his mother. Werner has studied this attitude and compares it with representations of Isis holding the child Horus on her lap. The analogy is certainly striking, but as the group on St Cuthbert's coffin shows the same disposition of the legs of the mother and child we are led to admit that this type of representation was known in the West long before the time when the Book of Kells was painted.[66] There is, however, a difference between the Durham Madonna and the Virgin and Child in the Book of Kells: the Child's head in the Kells picture is not shown *en face* but in profile and has no halo, while his mother has a large one stamped with three crosses. The Child in profile belongs to the most intimate representations of the Madonna, the Virgin of Tenderness, which became so popular in later Byzantine painting. It is especially characteristic of representations of the Nursing Madonna. In the Kells picture, the position of the hands of the Child deliberately stresses the affectionate note, and one may wonder if

64. Allen-Anderson, figs. 397A and 410. A slab from Brechin has been mentioned recently as a parallel (J. Richardson, *The Medieval Stone Carvers in Scotland*, Edinburgh, 1957, pp. 8 ff; see also Brown, *Northumbria-Kells*). The dating of that carving to the eighth century is very debatable. From the general attitude of the mother and child, it seems to be connected with a group of eleventh-century carvings from the north of England (T. D. Kendrick, *Late Saxon and Viking Art*, London, 1949, pp. 78–79; *Archaeologia*, 1973, pl. XLIV). It is probably an early version of this type, but not as early as the eighth century. See also C. Curle, 'The Chronology of the Early Christian Monuments of Scotland', *Proceedings of the Society of Antiquaries of Scotland*, 1939–40, pp. 60 ff.

65. F. Henry, *La sculpture irlandaise*, Paris, 1932, fig. 116, p. 151.

66. It is such a natural attitude for a woman holding a child that it can also be compared with a carving on a pagan sarcophagus in Rome (Grabar, *Christian Iconography*, fig. 93).

*Fig. 39 Maeseyck, Church of St Catherine, Fragments of Gospels, Evangelist*

down in front of him. The two upper angels hold their flabella with one hand and point with the other. Werner thinks that they point at their flabella. I am more inclined to think that they were imitated from angels placed lower in the picture and pointing at the Child, the painter forgetting to correct the now irrelevant gesture in his copy.[70]

The miniature is enclosed in a frame suggesting strongly that of a picture, which is broken only by a little panel containing six human busts, a device which is found on another page of the Book and seems intended to link together two facing decorated pages.

## The illustrations

As we have seen, only two pages of illustrations survive in the Book, the Arrest and the Temptation.

The representation of the Arrest of Christ in the Gospel of St Matthew is very stylized (pl. 45).[71] The scene is reduced to three figures, the two small soldiers looking flimsy and ineffective in comparison with the formidable figure they pretend to hold. This is obviously meant to stress the voluntary character of the Passion. There are, even at an early date, much more complex and crowded versions of the scene, for example that in Sant'Apollinare Nuovo in Ravenna (sixth century). The three figure simplification is based on an early Christian presentation which may have been transmitted to the West by one of the tiny pictures in the Gospels of St Augustine, a sixth-century Italian manuscript brought to England in the late sixth or early seventh century by missionaries sent from Rome.[72] This shows the same discrepancy of

the model followed slightly unfaithfully by the painter was not a picture of a Nursing Madonna. The great emphasis put on the modelling of the breasts by concentric circles would tend to indicate it. Meanwhile, the Virgin's head has not the relaxed flavour of some Coptic Madonnas and shows no evidence of human feeling. It is absolutely hieratic, with eyes staring at the onlooker and no attempt at bending towards the Child.

The presentation of the group is also worth studying. The chair belongs to that type of seat with animal terminals which we have examined *à propos* the portrait of St Matthew.[67] Three half-discs which fill the gaps between the angels at the top and on the sides may well be meant to suggest the shape of a cross with expanded terminals. But it is curious also that two of them, on the right and left, have parallels in similar half-discs attached to the two elongated animals forming the chair of St Mark in the Book of Lichfield.

Three of the angels hold flabella,[68] those circular fans used in Eastern liturgies to protect the chalice from dust and flies, which came very early to carry the symbolical meaning of purity and were represented for that reason on Insular pillars and Irish grave-slabs.[69] The lower angel on the left clings with both hands to the handle of his flabellum, while his counterpart on the right holds a flowering bough upside-

*Fig. 40 Monasterboice, Cross of Muiredach, Arrest of Christ*

67. It may be meant for the Throne of Solomon; see Schiller, *Iconography*, pp. 23 ff.

68. Cabrol-Leclercq, *Dictionnaire*, art. Flabellum.

69. P. Lionard, 'Early Irish Grave-Slabs', *P.R.I.A.*, 1961 (C), pp. 95 ff. (p. 137).

70. Henry, *Irish Art II*, pp. 79–80.

71. Réau, *Iconographie*, vol. II, 2, p. 434.

72. F. Wormald, *The Miniatures in the Gospel of St Augustine, Corpus Christi College, MS. 286*, Cambridge, 1954.

*Fig. 41 Cambridge, Corpus Christi College Library, MS 286 (Gospels of St Augustine),*
*Arrest of Christ*

size between Christ and the soldiers (fig. 41). But the whole atmosphere is different. The impressiveness of the figure of Christ in the Kells picture owes a great deal to the fiercely symmetrical treatment, each overemphasized fold on the right answering that on the left, and to the hieratic strangeness of the face with its staring blue eyes, golden curls and reddish beard. It is striking also that the two stiff bare arms held by the soldiers are already in a position suggestive of the Crucifixion, so that in every way the picture can act as a preface for the whole Passion. The soldiers, in fact, are not distinguished as such by their costume or by carrying weapons. In this the painter has followed the lead given him by the Gospels of St Augustine. It is curious to note that on the early tenth-century cross of Muiredach at Monasterboice, where the scene is also reduced to three figures, the soldiers wear a completely different costume from that of Christ and brandish swords (fig. 40).

The picture of the Temptation is much more complex in its presentation (pl. 68).[73] Christ, again very large, appears in

bust over the roof of the Temple. The Devil, a sooty and lanky form, stands in front of him on the side of the roof (pl. 110). Four angels hover about Christ's head, two of them being confined within triangular compartments in the top corners of the frame. Here are all the actors of the scene of the third Temptation as related by St Luke: 'And he [the Devil] led him to Jerusalem and there set him down on the pinnacle of the temple; if thou art the son of God, he said to him, cast thyself down from this to the earth; for it is written, He shall give his angels charge concerning thee, to keep thee safe, and they will hold thee up with their hands' (Luke IV, 9 ff.). But strangely enough, in the miniature, a crowd seems to witness the dialogue of Christ and the Devil. They are little bust-length figures seen in profile, nine of them immediately behind Christ, and in the lower part of the frame two groups of thirteen facing each other. It is debatable whether these last have any connection with a full-face bust holding two flabella in the Osiris pose[74] which appears in the door of the Temple. It has been suggested that the two lower groups and the figure in the door represent a Last Judgment – possibly because Christ in the Last Judgments carved on Irish crosses is shown in the Osiris pose. But if they are to be treated as separate from the Temptation scene, these figures are more likely to be an allusion to the events related by St Luke immediately after the Temptation, namely the preaching in Nazareth and Caphar-naum. Or, taking this picture as a preface to the whole narrative that follows, it might be a generalized description of Christ preaching during the three years of his public life. On the whole, it is more likely that the two groups below are a continuation of that to the right of Christ, and that together they form part of the description of a crowd of listeners.[75]

Though the Temptation of Christ is not a subject frequently represented before the Carolingian period, it is found in a psalter in the Library at Stuttgart, a manuscript originating from the north of France, probably from the region of Amiens,

*Fig. 42 Stuttgart Library, MS Bibl. fol. 23 (Stuttgart Psalter), Temptation of Christ on the*
*Mountain*

73. There are no early representations of this subject, which only appears in Continental as well as Byzantine art after 800. See Réau, *Iconographie*, vol. II, 2, pp. 304 ff.; Schiller, *Iconography*, pp. 143 ff.

74. For the Osiris pose, see below, p. 190.

75. This interpretation is made more likely by the fact that in the eleventh-century Vysehrad Gospels in Prague the pictures of the three temptations are accompanied by an image of Christ as Teacher between two angels (Schiller, *Iconography*, p. 144 and fig. 393).

*Fig. 43 Nuremberg, German Museum, Golden Evangeliar from Echternach, Temptation of Christ on the Temple*

and dating from the early ninth century (fig. 42).[76] In this case, what is represented is the Temptation on the Mountain and the devils are of the same totally black type as in the Book of Kells. On the other hand, in the Sacramentary of Drogo, a Carolingian manuscript, where the three temptations are shown as minute scenes encompassed in the curve of initials, the Devil is white-faced and wears a kind of black coat.[77] A late tenth-century manuscript, the Golden Gospels of Echternach in the Nuremberg Museum,[78] is much nearer to the Kells picture, as the Temple appears there also as a building seen from front and side at the same time, and the Devil is a totally black figure (fig. 43). That these black devils are of Byzantine origin is not only suggested by the constant use of that type in Byzantine manuscripts but also by the treatment of Temptation scenes in later mosaics of Byzantine inspiration or execution such as those at Monreale in Sicily and in St Mark's in Venice. The Temptation is not found either on Irish or English crosses.

A few features of the Kells picture are especially interesting: Christ wears a purple coat covered with groups of three dots similar to the coats of Our Lady (*f.* 7v: pl. 10) and of the figure in the door of the Temple (fig. 45).[79] But for the figure of Christ on the Temple, the coat is half covered by a striped, Oriental-looking drapery as if the divinity and majesty of Christ was partly veiled in this scene of his earthly life. The large halo which surrounds his head is practically identical with that of the Virgin on *f.* 7v – beaded edge, three crosses and a scatter of dots.

The angels are in two groups. The two immediately above the head of Christ are the equivalent of those seen beside Christ in the Stuttgart manuscript. Nearly symmetrical, their wings, which follow the stepped edges of the frame, form a sort of canopy above the head of Christ. The two other angels, as we have seen, are in triangular compartments. In contrast to the reverend, hushed atmosphere surrounding the lower group,

they gesticulate with great animation, each of them presenting a book, their figures tightly accommodated beside exuberant scrolls of foliage issuing from chalices (one of them shown sideways). These plants are similar to the vines supporting the two peacocks in the portrait of Christ and to the two potted plants in the tympanum above Christ in the scene of the Arrest. It looks as if various elements like haloes, pots and foliage, which are used in several pictures in the Book, had been borrowed repeatedly from the same model. It also seems likely that the two symmetrical plants play the part of emblems of Christ, illustrating his saying: *Ego sum vitis vera* ('I am the true vine', John XV, 1).

## The Osiris pose

Before going further, it may be useful to examine a type of figure pose which recurs with a startling persistency in the Book. The figure in the door of the Temple in the Temptation miniature is a good example (pl. 68; fig. 45): shown full-face, he holds two flabella whose handles are crossed at the height of

*Fig. 44 Lichfield Cathedral, Lichfield Gospels, portrait of St Luke*

76. E. T. de Wald, *The Stuttgart Psalter*, Princeton, 1930.

77. Koehler, *Karol. Miniat.*, vol. III, pl. 83.

78. P. Metz, *Das Goldene Evangelienbuch von Echternach im Germanischen National-Museum zu Nürnberg*, Munich, 1956.

79. Cf. a poem by the Irish ninth-century poet Sedulius Scottus, where

Christ is described as Christ wearing purple now reigns over
what high Begetter first created
blessed scion of the House of David
and our glory.
(Bieler, *Ireland*, p. 123; transl. J. Carney).

Fig. 45 *The Osiris pose: a Book of Kells, Temptation (f. 202v), detail; b Book of Kells, Symbols page of St John's Gospel (f. 290v), detail; c Cairo Museum, mummy case of Tutankhamun*

his waist and whose tops are a little above his shoulders. The arms are not crossed in this example, but the symbol of St Matthew in the four-symbols page preceding St John's Gospel (f. 290v: pl. 92; fig. 45) holds two books at the height of his shoulders with his arms crossed in front of him. The symbol of St Matthew on f. 1r (pl. 1; fig. 17) has his arms crossed, one of them brandishing a book, the other clutching a lock of his hair. Other examples in various attitudes can be quoted: the figure appearing above the monumental M of the *Argumentum* of Matthew, who holds two stems of foliage (pl. 12, top), the figure with two books at the top of f. 4r (pl. 7), etc. Ultimately crossed arms become a sort of obsession which dominates the pose or even the contortions of several figures, that in the Introductory page of St Mark's Gospel (pls. 51, 49), the fish-man in the genealogy (f. 201r: pl. 65), one of the angels in the *Una autem* page (f. 285r: pl. 89).

The remote origin of these figures is of course Osiris holding flail and crook-sceptre, Osiris the god who dies and revives, the judge of the dead, with whom the Egyptian dead were trying to identify themselves. As judge he is represented in the Book of the Dead holding his two insignia loosely, one on each shoulder, but in some cases his arms are tightly crossed on his breast.[80] This is, of course, the attitude of Tutankhamun-Osiris as shown on his mummy cases. It is tempting to think that these poses were transferred in Christian Egypt to representations of Christ and that from Coptic art they passed into Insular iconography. Unfortunately, as so often happens with problems of this kind, the link is missing and no Coptic intermediaries have been found so far.

In any case, it cannot be said to have been introduced directly into the repertory of the Book of Kells. That it was known before is clearly demonstrated by the imposing figure of St Luke holding cross and bough of foliage in the Lichfield

Gospels (fig. 44), and by the composite figure of the four symbols in the Trier Gospels. It is found also, from the beginning of the ninth century, on the Irish crosses where it serves for the representations of Christ as Judge. It occurs in England on the Alfred Jewel (late ninth century),[81] on the Anglo-Saxon Fuller brooch studied by Bruce-Mitford,[82] and on one of the crosses at Sandbach (Cheshire).[83] One or two icons showing Christ in this very impressive pose brought to some Western monasteries might have been enough to start this whole trail of various developments.

## The four angels

In a number of illuminated pages of the Book are found four winged figures probably meant for the four principal archangels: Michael, Gabriel, Raphael and Uriel.[84] Uriel, whose tradition was based on the apocryphal second book of Enoch,[85] began to be treated with some disfavour in the West from the eighth century on, but in the East, where Enoch II enjoyed a great popularity, invocation of the four archangels continued (they are called upon at the end of the Coptic mass). They are still found represented together in some parts of the West at a late date, and Martin Werner quotes in this respect a thirteenth-century Spanish illumination of the Virgin and Child surrounded by the four archangels identified by inscriptions.[86] So their presence in the Book of Kells is neither an archaism nor necessarily a sign of direct contact with the East.

The seven archangels are represented on St Cuthbert's coffin, Michael and Gabriel on one of the narrow sides, the others, Raphael, Uriel, etc., on one of the long sides (fig. 49). Michael carries a book in his left hand, Gabriel in his right. The others also carry books, except for one who holds a flowering bough on his right shoulder. The books may well be

80. E. Naville, *Das Egyptische Todtenbuch der XVIII bis zur XX Dynastie aus verschiedenen Urkunden*, Berlin, 1886; G. Kopakchy, *Le Livre des morts des anciens Egyptiens*, Paris, 1955. See Henry, *Irish Art II*, pp. 164–66.

81. J. Kirk, *The Alfred and the Minster Lovel Jewels*, Oxford, 1946.

82. R. Bruce-Mitford, 'Late Anglo-Saxon Disc Brooches', *Dark Age Britain*, London, 1956, pp. 171 ff., pl. XX.

83. Kendrick, *Anglo-Saxon Art*, p. 116, pl. XCV.

84. Cabrol-Leclercq, *Dictionnaire*, art. Anges. M. R. James, 'Names of Angels in Anglo-Saxon and other Documents', *Journal of the Theological Society*, 1909–10, pp. 569 ff. There is a mention of the seven archangels in the Irish *Saltair na Rann*, and a twelfth-century Irish prayer connects the

seven archangels with the seven days of the week (T. Ua Nualláin, 'A Prayer to the Archangels for each day of the week', *Eriu*, 1905, pp. 92–93). The 'unorthodox' archangels, condemned in the eighth century (745) did not disappear then; Uriel and Raguel, chiefly, are often found after that date. See G. Gaillard, 'La représentation des évangélistes à l'hypogée des Dunes', *Etudes mérovingiennes*, Paris, 1953, pp. 135–36.

85. W. R. Morphill and R. Charles, *The Book of the Secrets of Enoch*, Oxford, 1896; P. Perdrizet, 'L'archange Ouriel', *Seminarium Kondakovianum*, 1928, pp. 241 ff.

86. Werner, *Madonna and Child*, I, fig. 12.

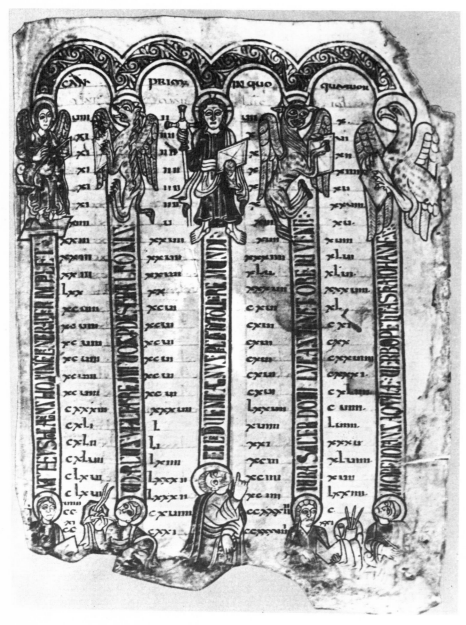

Fig. 46 Above: Autun, Municipal Library, MS 4, canon-table. Below: Jouarre, crypt, sarcophagus of Agilbertus (seventh century), Apocalyptic Vision

Fig. 47 Durham, Cathedral Museum, St Cuthbert's coffin, Apocalyptic Vision

*Fig. 48 Poitiers, Municipal Library, MS 17, Apocalyptic Vision*

*Fig. 49 Durham, Cathedral Museum, St Cuthbert's coffin, archangels (on the left, Raphael and Uriel)*

a borrowing from the figures of the Apostles on the other long side, and the bough may be an equivalent of the keys carried in exactly the same way by St Peter.

The four figures appear in the Virgin and Child page (*f.* 7v: pl. 10), the portrait of Christ (*f.* 32v: pl. 26), the Temp- tation (*f.* 202v: pl. 68) and the *Una autem* page (*f.* 285r: pl. 89). But in all cases there are unexpected variations. In *f.* 7v the two top figures have haloes, but not the others. We have seen that one holds a flowering bough upside down, while the three others hold flabella aloft. In *f.* 32v one figure carries a bough, but there are no flabella; in addition the figure with the bough does not seem to have wings, while the one below him is probably intended for a seraph, the virtuosity with which the wings are handled giving to a mere two pairs of wings the value of at least three. In the Temptation there are two adoring angels while the two others fuss around in the spandrels brandishing books amidst curling tendrils of vine. In *f.* 285r, four winged figures walk amidst the text or sit on its letters. They have one pair of wings each. The two top ones hold books, presenting them with their right hand on their left side; of the two below, one holds a bough over his right shoulder very much like the archangel on St Cuthbert's coffin, while the other does extraordinary gymnastics, holding a flabellum in both his right and left hands, his arms crossed at odd angles.

So books, flabella and sprouting boughs are attributes which can be distributed indiscriminately, it seems, amongst these four figures. The absence or excess of wings does not seem to worry the painters. It is worth noting, however, that there is never more than one flower-bearing angel and we have no example of more than two book-bearing angels on the same page.

## Other winged figures

Whether there is some relation between these groups and three angels appearing on the Monogram page (*f.* 34r: pl. 29) is hard to say. Two of them confront each other in a 'floating' attitude (pl. 106, top), like that of two angels carrying a medallion with the Lamb or the monogram of Christ. Each of them holds a book in one hand and a bough in the other; some distance further a third angel shown in full face holds two flowering stems which interlace with his wings.

Elsewhere there is only one angel, as on *f.* 183r (*Erat autem*, pl. 55), where a brightly coloured figure whose wings sparkle with lines and dots of all hues presides over the text of the Crucifixion (pl. 126).

But there seems to be sometimes a sort of euphoric feeling in the use of wings, and two of the winged figures appearing over the frames of the canon-tables are certainly not meant for angels but belong to a different series of representations altogether.

## The Trinity, the Godhead

Above several of the canon-tables there are weird, ghostly apparitions with or without wings, some with a large halo often marked with three crosses (*ff.* 1v, 2v, 3r, 4r: pls. 2, 4, 5, 7) and sometimes presenting one or even two books. They accompany the Evangelical symbols and seem to complement their meaning. The obvious interpretation of such figures is that they represent the Trinity or one of its persons whose story the Evangelists have told. In fact they form with the symbols below them an elusive *Majestas Domini*. There are further examples. On *f.* 12r (pl. 12) a figure with two boughs shows his head and feet behind the large M in the beginning of the *Argumentum* of Matthew: on *f.* 291v (pl. 94) a figure appears behind the frame of St John's portrait, and on *f.* 202r (pl. 67) another one peers over the tailpiece of the genealogy. This last is surely 'The Lord' mentioned just above and a similar explanation for the other figures is likely, the figure behind the frame of St John's portrait being fairly obviously the Word. They have in common the fact that they are not fully revealed to the eye; they appear over a frame or a letter, more suggested than described, the painter trying to convey by this device the unknowable character of God. This is an approach common in early Christian times but rare later. Perhaps, however, the bust of Christ painted just over the cross in the Valerianus Gospels, an Italian manuscript roughly contemporary with the Book of Kells, does supply a parallel.

## The symbols of the Evangelists

The origin of the bizarre figures symbolizing each of the Evangelists is twofold. Ezekiel tells of having a vision of a great cloud filled with fire, 'and there in the heart of it, in the very heart of the fire, was a glow like amber, that enclosed four

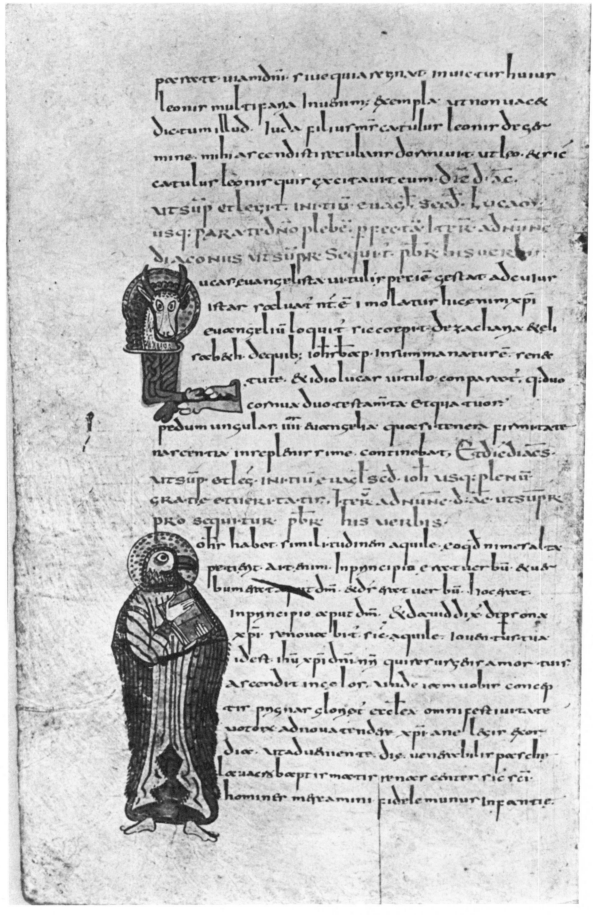

*Fig. 50 Paris, National Library, MS Lat. 12048 (Sacramentary of Gellone), page of text*

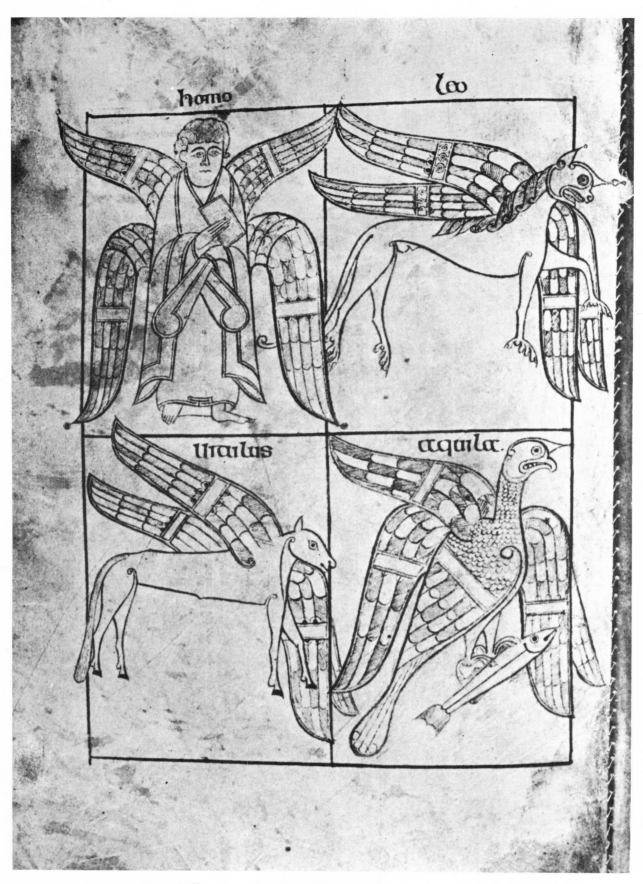

homo                    leo

uitulus                 aquila

living figures. These were human in appearance but each had
four faces and two pairs of wings. . . . As for the appearance of
their faces, each had the face of a man, yet each of the four
looked like a lion when seen from the right, like an ox when
seen from the left, like an eagle when seen from above' (Ezekiel
I, 4 ff.). Above these hovers a figure sitting on a throne and
surrounded by a light like a rainbow. The author of the
Apocalypse describes a vision on the same pattern: 'And all at

once I was in a trance and saw where a throne stood in heaven
and one sat there enthroned. . . . Round the throne itself were
four living figures that had eyes everywhere to see before them
and behind them. The first figure was that of a lion, the
second that of an ox, the third had a man's look and the fourth
was that of an eagle in flight. Each of the four figures had six
wings . . . ; day and night they cried unceasingly, Holy, holy,
holy is the Lord God, the Almighty who ever was, and is and

is still to come' (Ap. IV, 2ff.). Gradually, the tremendous beasts of the visions were tamed by the commentators and became the identifying symbols of the four Evangelists,[87] until the Middle Ages sometimes irreverently turned them into household pets. But at the stage at which we are, the great commotion of the fiery cloud still seems to linger about them. It was some time before they got definitively attributed, the man to Matthew, as his Gospel starts with the enumeration of the human ancestry of Christ, the lion to Mark, because in the beginning of his Gospel is quoted the prophecy of Isaiah about 'the voice crying in the desert', the calf or ox to Luke whose Gospel starts with the story of Zacharias' sacrifice, and the eagle to John who soars in his first words to great heights, like the eagle which is not afraid to fly straight towards the sun.

Their degree of humanity or animality varies from human figures with animal heads to complete animals, sometimes with human hands. At the time in the early Middle Ages when the Book of Kells was decorated the Vision is often depicted, with the 'figure' on the throne surrounded by the four beasts. This is the *Majestas Domini* of which we have seen that there is no straightforward version in the Book. By this time too they appear sometimes as headings for the lists in the canon-tables, a use which seems in a way to belittle their supernatural character and turn them flatly to a practical, almost a mnemonic function. In the hands of the painters of the Book of Kells, however, this danger is brilliantly avoided and the symbols retain their wild, unearthly quality. They are perhaps the most

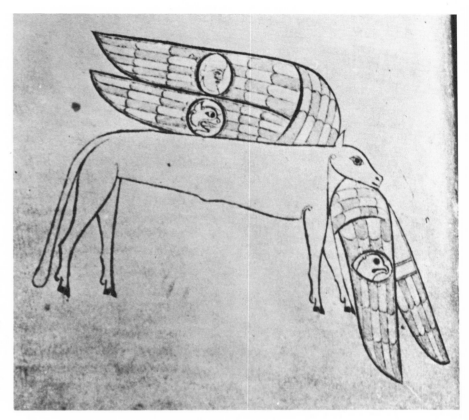

*Fig. 53 Dublin, Trinity College Library, MS 52 (Book of Armagh), symbol of St Luke*

striking element in the decoration of the Book, a constant leitmotif running through the large illustrated pages, as Giraldus Cambrensis so rightly observed.

They are found on the first surviving page as a sort of preface to the canon-tables, within most of these tables them-selves and, for each of the Gospels except Luke, on a page with all four of them shown together.

The first page (*f.* 1r: pl. 1) is remarkable from several points of view. As we have seen, it presents the Evangelists in a highly unusual order, perhaps reading from right to left. This would, however, become more intelligible if there was at the top of the page a figure in bust similar to those in the canon-tables. The symbols would then seem to be moving towards it, waving their books. This figure may have existed. There are obviously traces of painting above the frame. But the condition of the leaf is such that the presence of a figure is not absolutely certain.

The three animal symbols appear here under a rare aspect: they are animal to the point of showing each a hind leg which could leave no doubt on the subject, but they have human hands. This may be an attempt to illustrate the rather obscure statement of Ezekiel: 'Either leg was straight-formed, yet ended in a calf's hoof . . . human arms showed beneath the wings' (Ezekiel I, 7–8). A little further in the Book (*f.* 5r: pl. 9) St John is again represented by an eagle with human hands. These are not properly speaking anthropomorphic symbols, i.e. human figures with animal heads of the type studied in detail by René Crozet.[88] They have been called, aptly but

*Fig. 52 Composite symbols of St Luke in the Book of Kells (ff. 1v and 2v)*

87. Mâle, *Gothic image*, pp. 36 ff.; Réau, *Iconographie*, vol. II, 2, pp. 44 ff.
88. R. Crozet, 'Les quatre évangélistes et leurs symboles, assimilation et adaptations', *Les cahiers techniques de l'art*, 1962.

*Fig. 54, Munich, Library, MS 4452 (from Bamberg Cathedral), symbol of St Luke with the Resurrection*

ECCE LEO FORTIS·TRANSIT DIS CRIMINA MORTIS·

awkwardly, 'zoanthropomorphic symbols'. 'Symbols with human hands' might be less cumbersome.

This type of representation is much less common than the symbols in completely animal form or the symbols in human form with animal heads. This seems to be their only occurrence in Insular manuscripts, indicating a wider range of contacts for the Book of Kells than for other Insular books. Strangely enough, the group of manuscripts from northern France whose relations with Insular manuscripts we have already discussed seems to prefer human symbols with animal heads. These are found in the manuscript from Sainte Croix at Poitiers and the Sacramentary of Gellone (figs. 48, 50). The more usual symbols in completely animal shape occur in the two Insular manuscripts which have symbol canon-tables, the fragment at Maeseyck and the Barberini Gospels (fig. 16). In the latter, though the symbols, shown in busts, clearly have animal heads and paws or claws, their shoulders are draped. In the Book of Kells, apart from the exceptions mentioned above, the symbols are shown right through the Book in completely animal form.

In the canon-tables, up to *f.* 4r the symbol of St Matthew is always shown as an angel holding a book and turned towards the right to follow the direction of the writing below. Only on *f.* 5r (pl. 9) – an anomalous composition anyway – does he appear holding aloft a flabellum like some of the archangels. The three animal symbols are without books, but their appearance is not always conventional. On *f.* 1v (pl. 2; fig. 52) the symbol of St Luke is an extremely composite creature, winged and more like an angry cockerel than a meek sacrificial calf, though he has the appropriate head and hoofs. The third symbol on *f.* 2v (pl. 4) is no less surprising: it has the body, wings and talons of an eagle and the head of a calf (fig. 52). This is sometimes explained as an attempt to amend the errors of the text below, but the composite figure on *f.* 1v where no such explanation is necessary points rather to an effort towards

recapturing something of the shifting quality of the creatures described by Ezekiel.

This tendency to alter the normal aspect of the calf may also reflect a tradition clearly formulated by Honorius Augusto-dunensis. The four beasts are there interpreted as representing four stages of the life of Christ: birth, death, resurrection and ascension to heaven (*Christus erat homo nascendo, vitulus moriendo, leo resurgendo, aquila ascendendo*, says Honorius: Christ was a man in his birth, a calf in his dying, a lion in his resurrection, an eagle in his ascending).[89] This symbolism is manifest in twelfth-century lectionaries and is frequent in Romanesque and Gothic art. But it is certainly much older as shows an Ottonian manuscript of *c.* 1000 in Bamberg where the Man is accompanied by a picture of the Nativity, the Lion by the Resurrection (fig. 54), the Calf by the Crucifixion and the Eagle by the Ascension.[90] So these various efforts at disguising the calf may have a deeper reason. When he is turned into a composite being with features of the lion and the eagle, he is really meant for Christ dead, rising again and ascending to heaven. This may also explain the strange lay-out of the Introductory page of St Luke's Gospel, the *Quoniam* (pl. 61), where a lion partly hidden by the frame appears above and below it, as elusive in its presentation as the partly-hidden figures of God we have examined earlier. Is this not the Christ of the Resurrection taking the place, on that page where he is nowhere represented, of the sacrificial calf one would have expected?

The four-symbol pages which precede the Gospels show not only a different arrangement each time but a different mood also. They are in the normal tradition of the Insular Gospel-books and are found in the Book of Durrow (late seventh century), the Book of Lichfield (early eighth) and the Book of Armagh (early ninth; fig. 51). But in each of these there is only one such page for the whole book, while each Gospel is introduced by the appropriate symbol (Durrow and Armagh[91])

89. *Patr. Lat.* 172, col. 956.
90. Munich Library, MS 4452; Mâle, *Gothic Image*, p. 37, n. 1; Grabar, *Christian Iconography*, fig. 293.

91. The Book of Armagh has no page with the symbol of Matthew, as the four symbols page replaces it.

or by the portraits of the Evangelists (Lichfield). Kells, reaching a pitch of lavishness unknown before or after in Insular manuscripts, was planned with both a four-symbols page and a portrait at the beginning of each Gospel.

The page at the beginning of St Matthew is presented in the simplest way, with each symbol enclosed in a rectangular compartment (f. 27v: pl. 20). This gives it a kinship with the Lichfield page, but the Kells 'beasts' have haloes with dots or crosses and the red beaded border of the haloes given to the Virgin and to Christ in ff. 7v and 202v (pls. 10, 68). The symbol of St Matthew holds a cross and that of St John stands on a little rectangular platform or footstool which may be meant for a book (pls. 19, 91).

The page which opens St Mark's Gospel (f. 129v: pl. 50) is much more complex. It is also divided into four rectangular compartments. But inside these, the symbols are each almost completely contained in circular haloes penetrated however by the pairs of flabella they hold. In the intervals between halo and rectangle some of the other symbols are shown. One would expect these additional symbols to be complementary to that which is inside the halo, but this is not always the case. A detailed description of each compartment will make this clear: (1) a winged human figure in the halo, with a kind of elaborate bird's tail interlaced with the halo; above, another winged human figure;[92] (2) a winged lion in the halo; below, a winged calf and an eagle; (3) a winged calf in the halo; above, an eagle and another winged calf; (4) an eagle in the halo, its tail protruding outside; a lion and a winged calf below. Allusions in representations of one symbol to the other three are to be found in the Book of Armagh (fig. 53), where small medallions with the heads of the other symbols are drawn on the wings of the calf and the eagle. But in that case the system is perfectly straightforward. The Kells page presents us with something of a much more elusive nature where the symbolism of death (calf), resurrection (lion) and ascension (eagle) is probably the essential factor.

The symbols page at the beginning of St John's Gospel is by far the most magnificent and imaginative of the three (f. 290v: pl. 92). It is divided into four triangular spaces by a saltire cross ending in dragon heads. The symbols are disposed anti-clockwise. St Matthew's symbol, at the top, with two pairs of wings and no halo, holds two books in the Osiris pose and dominates the composition. The lion on the left, also it seems with two pairs of wings, could easily be mistaken for a bird if it was not for its fierce, roaring head. The splendid purple eagle on the right looks over its shoulder (pl. 111, bottom), while the acid-green calf with two little pointed horns has only one pair of wings (pl. 111, top).

So the greatest diversity governs the representation of these symbols in the Book of Kells: they may or may not have haloes or carry flabella. The man and occasionally the beasts may carry a book or even two books. They may transfer certain aspects of their appearance to each other. But, whatever

the changes, they never appear as human figures wearing animal heads. Either the three beasts are resolutely animal, or they have no more than human hands and arms, and this perhaps only in order to be better able to carry a book.

The other remarkable thing about them is that they never seem to appear as they do in the Visions, supporting and accompanying the 'figure of light', at least in a coherent and unambiguous composition. But we have seen that there are in some of the canon-tables elements of a 'Christ in Majesty', though presented in an unusual way. And one may wonder whether the carefully organized cross-shaped compartments in the inside frames of the symbol-pages of Matthew and Mark are not intended to suggest the missing central figure. In the saltire symbol-page (pl. 92) the monogram of Christ – Chi-Rho, XP – is probably implied, each curved dragon head forming a Rho. The replacement of the central figure by a flaming monogram is an early Christian device, found for example in the mosaic of the vault in the archepiscopal chapel at Ravenna. It seems to have been adapted here in an even more mysterious and secretive way, and the dragon heads are probably meant for lions, symbols of the Resurrection.

## The Chi-Rho page

The strangest perhaps of all the pages in the Book is that in which the monogram of the Greek form of Christ's name (Chi-Rho, XP) constitutes all the decoration, leaving room for only a small line of ordinary writing (f. 34r: pl. 29). The Chi spreads widely, hardly contained by the suggestion of a frame on the right. It is outlined in mauve and filled with minute networks of birds, various animals and, in the centre, a tight plaiting of human figures and birds. The letter flames out in all directions in a frenzy of spirals of many kinds (pl. 106, bottom). In the intervals of this riot of circles appear the three angels we have already examined (pl. 106, top), two delicately painted moths or butterflies and, in the lower part of the page, an otter holding a fish in its mouth beside a strange group of animals which has generally been described as two cats and four mice, two of them nibbling at a cross-inscribed disc (pl. 107, bottom). The small animals are more likely to be kittens with their parents, the large cats holding two of the smaller ones by the tail. The moths seem to be engaged in eating a lozenge,[93] while the fish held by the otter is the early Christian symbol of Christ which keeps reappearing in the Book. The disc is probably meant for a host or eucharistic bread. So the otter, the moths and the young cats are probably emblems of the faithful partaking of the Eucharist. Why this unexpected choice of symbolic animals? We cannot say, but through this page where we hold a guiding line to the symbolic intentions of the painter, however tenuous, it may be, we can at least become conscious of the wealth of now lost meanings which hides under the acrobatic feats of the animal initials and the 'turn-in-the-path'.

---

92. It is impossible to know to which of the figures the feathery tail belongs.

93. There are indications that the lozenge is a Christian symbol, though its exact meaning is hard to define. See Cabrol-Leclercq, *Dictionnaire*, art. Losange. The Virgin in the Book of Kells, as in several medieval figurations, wears a lozenge-shaped brooch. (It is true that one of the soldiers in the Arrest of Christ on the Cross of Muiredach at Monasterboice also wears one, but then on some of the Irish crosses the soldiers have haloes, probably by a similar confusion.)

We have already considered the general lay-out of the decoration in the genealogy. Some of it is probably purely ornamental, but there are also elements which have a definite meaning. One may wonder how to interpret the human figure which appears very prominently at the top of the *Qui fuit* series (f. 200r: pl. 63). But on f. 201v (pl. 66) there are several human figures looking as if they were giving a sort of impudent high kick (pl. 117); the last one holds a large flowering bough in his hand and though the name of Jesse, David's father, is listed on the preceding page (f. 201r: pl. 65), it is most probably he who is meant here, accompanied by some of his descendants. This would be one of the earliest surviving representations of the ancestor of whom the prophet Isaiah had said: *Egredietur virga de radice Jesse et flos de radice ejus ascendet* ('from the stock of Jesse a scion shall burgeon yet, out of his roots a flower shall spring'; Isaiah XI, 1). From early times – and the interpretation is helped by the verses that follow in Isaiah – the flower had been understood as meaning Christ and the stem as Mary, descendant of David.[94] From the twelfth century onwards large trees of Jesse carrying in their branches several of the ancestors and finally Mary and Christ will spread in the windows of Romanesque and Gothic churches. But a little earlier the representations are simpler: either the tree is no more than a stem carrying seven medallions with seven doves – the gifts of the Holy Ghost – or the ancestors of Christ are shown each holding a bough. On the early twelfth-century façade of the church of Notre-Dame-la-grande in Poitiers, Jesse is represented by a figure with a stem of foliage spreading above his head. It is not known where this pictorial theme originated, though it may have been in Byzantine art.

On the same page (f. 201v), the little human figure holding a cup who sits on the end of Abraham's name is no doubt Melchisedek. On f. 201r (pl. 65), the name 'Iona' probably suggested the fish-human figure who grasps the end of the T of the *fuit* on Iona's line. But can we go further and identify the six scraggy fowl above and below the fish-man,[95] or the little warrior on f. 200r (pl. 63)?[96] Hardly.

The genealogy ends (pl. 67) with *Adam qui fuit Domini* (Adam, son of the Lord); then comes as a tail-piece a figure in human shape appearing behind a large rectangular panel with two birds on one side and a double scroll of vine on the other, obviously a representation of the Lord mentioned above (without halo, but then haloes are optional in the Book). The birds (pl. 109, top) are a stylized version of the two peacocks on f. 32v (pl. 26) which, as we have seen, are emblems of Christ, and the vine issuing from a chalice-shaped vase completes the symbol (pl. 109, bottom).

The pages of decorative text which inaugurate each of the Gospels are not only masterpieces of combinations of lines and colours, they also contain a few figures which may not be pure ornament. We are already aware of the undercurrents of hidden meaning which run through the Book and have to be explored patiently, though very cautiously. So let us look at these pages one by one.

First, the Introductory page of St Matthew, *Liber generationis* (f. 29r: pls. 23, 104). Amidst the ornament of this page are three human figures. One has a halo and carries a book in front of him. It may be another representation of the Evangelist, a small-scale echo of the portrait on the opposite page (f. 28v: pl. 22). But what of the angel floating in a purple sky (at the left in pl. 104)? Most probably it is the symbol of St Matthew which often tends to play the part of an inspiring angel and is here shown rushing towards the Evangelist. An important point, as this feature recurs in two other Introductory pages, is that the frame of the page ends with a dragon or lion head; here it is shown with a sort of scaly halo. The large figure on the left presenting a book can hardly be the Evangelist again and I am tempted to see in him the donor of the Book or somebody closely connected with its production.[97] He wears the little black shoes, probably in current use, seen on the feet of some of the Evangelists in the Book of Dimma and the Book of Mac Durnan (fig. 33). Sullivan thought that he was a later addition, which does not seem to make sense, as he is an essential part of the composition of the page.

The beginning of St Mark's Gospel, *Initium Evangelii IHU XPI* (f. 130r: pl. 51) has a large figure dressed in a sort of tightly fitting knitted costume. He is swept by the movement of the ornament and the jaws of the lion's head ending the frame of the page are interlaced with him (pl. 49). In a contortion derived from the Osiris pose he holds with one hand the tongue of the lion, with the other the spiral connected both with his own beard and with two small peacocks. This is most probably an unexpected version of the Evangelist and his symbol, irreverent perhaps to our stilted minds, though it must have looked simple and commonplace to the freer imagination of the painter.

The beginning of St Luke, *Quoniam* (f. 188r: pl. 61), unusual in its presentation and style, does not seem to include any allusion to the Evangelist and his symbol. We have seen that it has in fact a lion partly hidden by the frame. It has also a number of small human figures half falling amidst the letters (pl. 114), who seem dead or asleep. As they are exactly above the lion, symbol of the resurrected Christ, the possibility that this could be an allusion to the Harrowing of Hell or Descent

---

94. A. Watson, *The early Iconography of the Tree of Jesse*, Oxford, 1934; Réau, *Iconographie*, vol. II, 2, pp. 129 ff.; Schiller, *Iconography*, pp. 15 ff. One of the earliest surviving attempts at illustrating the text of Isaiah is found in the Lorsch Gospels (early ninth century), where in the genealogy two of the figures hold palm-like boughs: see Koehler, *Karol. Miniat.*, vol. II, pls. 91–166.

95. Unless we have here the seven gifts of the Holy Ghost figured by doves on early trees of Jesse, the fish-man alluding to Jonah standing perhaps for fortitude. They are assimilated to the seven spirits which, according to Isaiah (II, 2), were to rest upon the Messiah, and in later trees of Jesse they form a sort of halo around the head of Christ.

96. Though in the early twelfth-century *Vitae Sanctorum* from Citeaux in Dijon Library the tree of Jesse is surrounded by four prefigurations, one of them being Gideon's fleece, and Gideon is represented with lance and shield. But to accept this interpretation and the preceding one it would be necessary to postulate the existence of more fully-developed early figurations of the theme than any which have survived.

97. Donors are frequently represented from an early date in mural paintings and mosaics. For a portrait of a donor in a manuscript roughly contemporary with the Book of Kells, see a manuscript from Vercelli in Hubert-Porcher-Volbach, fig. 162.

*Fig. 55 Oxford, Bodleian Library, MS Auct.D.II.19 (Book of Mac Regol), Introductory
page of St Matthew's Gospel (Liber)*

*Fig. 56 Stockholm, Royal Library, MS 155 (Codex Aureus), canon-table*

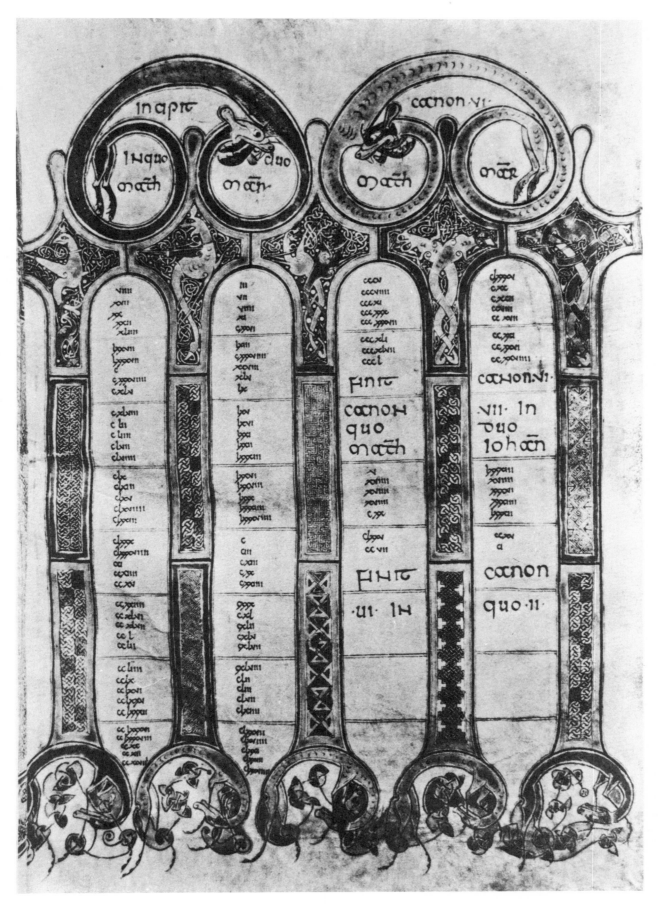

*Fig. 57 Leningrad, State Public Library, MS Lat.F.V.I.No. 8, canon-table*

into Limbo comes to mind.[98] The scene is of course frequently represented in Byzantine painting, though in a much more matter-of-fact way.

With folio 292r (pl. 95), the beginning of St John, *In Principio erat Verbum*, we return to the type of construction used in the opening of Matthew and Mark. John the Evangelist seems to be represented at the top right, holding a chalice, one of his most usual emblems, and is faced by a dragon or lion head emerging from the frame. The human figure in full face dressed in a purple cloak, holding a book and sitting on a throne draped in light is likely to be a representation of the Word, and consequently a sort of illustration of the text of the page.

It is noteworthy that all four Introductory pages (pls. 23, 51, 61, 95) have a lion or a lion head. What we have seen of the multiple interpretations of the lion makes this perhaps easier to understand. In St Mark (pl. 51), the lion is more especially the symbol of the Evangelist, but that it means Christ at the same time is indicated by the presence of the two peacocks. In the three other Gospels it means Christ, more especially the resurrected Christ.

## The architectural elements

The illustrations of the Book of Kells include several elements of architecture – arcades in the canon-tables, arches above the portrait of Christ, that of St Matthew and the scene of the Arrest – and a representation of one whole building, the Temple of Jerusalem in the Temptation scene.

Arcades as a frame for the comparative lists of the Gospels are not an invention of the painters of the Book of Kells. As we have seen, they are devices of late Antique origin which were adapted by Insular artists in various ways. In the Book of Lindisfarne they are of an elegant Insular academism which retains only the outline of columns, capitals and arches. It is like the shadow of classical arcades on which the Insular bestiary has crept. The first canon of the Barberini Gospel-book (fig. 16) is also of the silhouette type, but with some vivid details and symbols of the Evangelists under the arches. Only the Leningrad Gospels indulge in the full logic of Insular decoration (fig. 57), replacing the column bases and arches with curled animals and ignoring the capitals.[99] At the other extreme are the canons of the Stockholm Codex Aureus (fig. 56), where the capitals in some pages still have a good semblance of acanthus leaves and the bases a memory of classical mouldings. But on other pages, as also in the Cotton Psalter Vespasian A.I, which has a type of arch filled with spirals similar to that in the Codex Aureus, capitals and column bases have turned into discs, as they have in some canon-pages of the Book of Kells. These two manuscripts, copied in Canterbury in the eighth century, show an aspect of the interpenetration of the classical and Insular styles which is not very far from that found in some of the canons of the

Book of Kells. Though the proportions of classical architecture and some of its details are completely ignored, a certain feeling for volume and structure survive, a robustness alien to the shadow-play of the Lindisfarne Gospels. This is the feeling given by the Kells canons up to folio 4r (pls. 2–7), in spite of square or rounded bases and odd capitals. The models may have been classical or Byzantine. (The shape of some of the capitals would in fact point to Byzantine sources: ff. 2v and 3r, pls. 4, 5). Their vigorous inspiration can still be felt, but the painter, steeped in the vision of the Insular artist, turns them to his own purpose. It is more than probable that the man who was thus drawing columns had never seen one, as the absence of columns is a feature of Irish and Scottish church building at the time.[100] It is all the more surprising that in several cases he achieved an almost convincing appearance. But this unfamiliarity probably explains the extreme oddity of the bent columns in the portraits of Christ and of St Matthew (pls. 26, 22), and the breaking up of the columns into nearly disconnected patterns in the Arrest (pl. 45).

The miniature of the Temple is in many ways more interesting and original (pl. 68; fig. 58). It shows the front of a building framed by two majestic antae and the beams of a low-reaching roof with a rectangular door in the middle. But, as in most pre-Gothic representations of buildings, a second angle of vision is introduced and the roof is shown in profile, its master beam decorated at both ends by heart-shaped animal carvings. Roof and wall are covered with regular patterns of various colours which may well imitate a decoration in painted shingle or lead. In fact, practically all the features of the building are surprisingly real and can be paralleled by surviving features of Irish churches: the antae, the animal finials, the rectangular door; shingle and lead coverings are mentioned in texts. So here it seems that the artist, instead of trying to imitate the scarcely intelligible intricacies of classical architecture, has drawn on his own experience and given us a fairly accurate picture of a type of building with which he was familiar.

*Fig. 58 Book of Kells, Temptation (f. 202v), detail: the Temple of Jerusalem*

---

98. There is an incomplete text of the Harrowing of Hell (*Descensus ad Inferna*) on the last two pages of the Book of Cerne (E. Bishop, *Liturgica Historica*, Oxford, 1918, pp. 173 ff. and 192 ff.).

99. The same attitude of complete disregard for the architectural nature of the arcades is found in the Gospel-book in Essen Cathedral and in a manuscript which has Insular features, though it originates from a Conti-

nental scriptorium, MS 4 in the Municipal Library at Autun (fig. 46).

100. There are no columns in any of the surviving early Irish stone churches and there is no proof of the existence of wooden columns in Ireland or Scotland at the time. Even the Saxon 'balusters' which decorated the churches of Jarrow and Wearmouth can hardly be dignified with the name of columns.

# THE REPERTOIRE OF
# ORNAMENT

The ornament in the Book of Kells, as in most Insular manu-scripts, plays an unusually important role, not only because of its extent but also because of its variety and the different ways in which each pattern can be used.

While in many more or less contemporary Continental manuscripts fish and bird patterns, with a few interlacings or varieties of the acanthus leaf, form the basis of a monotonous if quite effective decoration, there is in our manuscript a constant shifting from spiral to interlacing, from key-pattern to animal or human interweavings; a whole zoo of snakes, dragons, fish, cats and birds passes across the pages, combining with more linear ornament, bending to the shape of letters, merging into a variety of other motifs and emerging out of them again.

The elements of this proliferation are roughly the same as in many other Insular manuscripts. However the frequent use of foliage in the Book of Kells, both inside the ornamental frames and in the text decoration, is unusual. The Barberini Gospels present the only parallel in this respect.[101] The use of human interlacing, too, while not unknown elsewhere (it appears in the Turin Gospels and in MS 1395 in the St Gall Library; figs. 30, 59), remains rare and sporadic outside the Book. But as soon as one turns its pages it meets the eye every-where and must be considered among the staple ornaments.

Not only are there new or rare patterns in the Book, but most of the ornament, as Sullivan very pertinently remarked, appears there in its most sophisticated forms, in what could be described as a late and elaborated, though in no way degenerate phase. The strong tendency of the different elements to combine together, forming in some cases a continuous, ever-shifting pattern, is also the mark of a time when all the motifs have been accepted and absorbed to a point where they come together like the letters of a word or the words of a sentence.

The *spiral* is the oldest ornament in Insular decoration. It is known and constantly used in pre-Roman Britain as well as in pre-Christian Ireland and Scotland, as part of the curvi-linear patterns which seem to have been favoured by the Celts and derived by them from classical palmettes and scrolls. It probably also owes a debt to solar patterns such as the helix. From early Christian metal objects it was transferred to the pages of manuscripts. It appears thus in the initials of the Cathach of St Columba (fig. 2), and on a carpet-page and some large initials in the Book of Durrow (fig. 24). At that

stage it is still very simple. The centres of some of the swirls are filled with little animal heads and very plain patterns of one or three leaves or a triangle are used to connect the curves. For the most part it remains close to pure geometry, the curves being sometimes drawn with compasses from double centres. The spirals of the Lichfield Gospels are hardly more elaborate (fig. 61). In the Book of Lindisfarne, the very simple grid used in construction is sometimes revealed by pricked centres which can be seen on the reverse of the page. Except for the use of a more free-hand drawing, St Gall MS 51 and the Book of Mac Regol have spirals of the same straightforward and uncompli-cated type (figs. 27, 55). But with the Book of Kells the treatment of the motif changes beyond recognition, the spiral centres becoming discs which themselves contain other discs filled with little human acrobats or interlace or sometimes with more spirals (see for example pls. 27, 29, 104–106).[102] The feeling is of a creeping plant spreading, displaying large flowers and spreading again. And this is not just a simile. The insistence on the vegetable aspect of the motif is very striking, as if it were going back to one of its remote origins, the plant scroll. Sometimes one may wonder if the illuminator is not using it as a sort of stylized vine: the way in which the spirals sprout on every side of the monogram of Christ makes this hypothesis tempting (pl. 29).

*Interlacing* also belongs to the stock in trade of Insular illumination, whatever its ultimate source – imitation of Coptic manuscripts, influence of Saxon jewellery, or, as Sir Thomas Kendrick would have it, imitation of Roman pavements. At a very early time in the Near East it was a stylized representation of running water, and something of its origin may still have been perceived by the illuminator and may have influenced the widespread use of the pattern. It appears in the Book of Durrow and on some stone monuments in the neighbourhood of Derry in the form of wide ribbons sometimes following a strange angular course. But a thin thread-like grille soon took the place of this first version, which is scarcely ever met with later. In the Book of Kells there is little trace of it and most interlacings are sharp and metallic-looking. They never, however, show any great virtuosity, conforming in this to the interlacing on Irish crosses and metalwork. The Turin manuscript, on the other hand, has a page of astounding brio and complexity where the lines of the

---

101. The Cuthbrecht Evangeliar in Vienna National Library (MS 1224), has some foliage ornament which is not very different from that in the Book of Kells; for an initial with foliage ornament in the Leningrad Bede, which Lowe dates 731–35 and attributes to Jarrow-Wearmouth,

see Meyer Shapiro, 'The Decoration of the Leningrad Manuscript of Bede', *Scriptorium*, 1958, pp. 191 ff.

102. 'St John's Cross' at Iona also has a most complicated treatment of spirals.

*Fig. 59 St Gall, Cathedral Library, MS 1395, detail of ornamental page*

thread form great wheels recalling the elaborate interweavings on the Scottish slabs.[103]

The tendency to combine and run various patterns into each other, which we have noted, is especially pronounced with spirals and interlacing. A three-fold knot or a plait is frequently a means of linking spirals together, and this with such ease and spontaneity that the motifs seem, in the mind of the artist, to have simply fused into a more complex one (pls. 105, 107, 113).

There are a number of *angular patterns*, many of which can be classified as step-patterns, while others, more elaborate and based on the combination of little hooked motifs, are better described as key-patterns. Some of them are so simple that they could have been invented spontaneously in different places. Others, more complicated, can be traced to classical or Oriental models. The key-pattern is especially common in the decoration of the Book of Kells and in the canon-tables it shares popularity with spirals, interlacing and animal or human interlacing (pls. 4, 5). This is all the more surprising as it is a monotonous, tedious ornament, not much susceptible to change or inventions. Being the most inert of the whole range of ornament in the manuscript, its almost complete absence from the most intricate pages such as the Chi-Rho and eight-circles pages (*ff.* 33r and 34r: pls. 27, 29) is not surprising.

There is, however, one example of this ornament which has its importance. The circular bases of the columns framing the figure of Christ on *f.* 32v (pl. 26) and a capital on folio 3r (pl. 5) each have a sort of labyrinth pattern which has equivalents on the terminals of some silver Hiberno-Viking brooches of the ninth century (fig. 60). This can hardly be a coincidence, as the design is distinctive, and so this detail supplies a useful hint as to the date of the manuscript.[104]

There is a whole category of decorative elements, *zoomorphic* or *human* in its component parts, which is of an infinitely more elusive nature, richer and more varied in its

effects, liable to all sorts of changes, capable of passing from the most straightforward likenesses to strangely arbitrary deformations. Men, fantastic animals, snakes, dragons, lions, cats and birds may be found completely disciplined and organized, following the grid of an interlacing, inside some of the frames of a large composition, but they may also, liberated from that box-like presentation, be simply folded to the shape of an initial, or else, regaining the maximum of freedom, they may walk between the lines of the text or indicate the direction in which it is to be read. Thus they may appear sometimes as a real human, a prancing beast or a bird flying across the page, though tenuous changes and a rhythmic repetition of attitudes are enough to integrate them into the world of patterns governed by the rules of ornament.

Take human figures for example. On *f.* 188r (pl. 61, the beginning of St Luke), at the top right of the large initial little men face each other in groups of two, their legs, arms and hair treated as the elements of an interlacing. But what of the other men, further down, who crowd between and across the smaller letters (pl. 114)? We have seen that they have perhaps a definite meaning. They are however very strange in their attitudes, on the sharp edge between ornament proper and the dream of the scribe on his text. Again, take that beast which can only be described as a dragon-lion-cat because of its protean but always feline character. It can be the Lion of Judah. It is more often the lion, symbol of St Mark, a creature still glowing from the glory of the Vision. As such we have seen it on the various pages of symbols and on the canon-

*Fig. 60 Discs with angular patterns: a silver brooch, Dublin, National Museum; b, c Book of Kells (ff. 32v, 3r); d Belfast, Ulster Museum, trial-piece from Lissue*

103. Henry, *Irish Art II*, pl. 38; for the Scottish slabs, see Allen-Anderson, *passim*.

104. *Christian Art in Ancient Ireland*, I (ed. A. Mahr), Dublin, 1932.

tables. It may or may not have a halo and wings, but it always has a mane of spiral locks, slender paws with claws and that strange head with pointed ears, a large eye and a mouth generally well supplied with fangs. But similar heads may sprout at the end of a frame or be part of the structure of the page. The canon-page on *f.* 5r (pl. 9), for example, has, as one of the two animal-symbols in the tympanum, a most elegant lion (pl. 101, top), but, to its right and left, two lion or dragon heads bite the smaller arches and they have the same curly mane as the symbol beast. We have seen that it can also be a symbol of the resurrected Christ, and that in the Introductory pages these various meanings are used together or separately. On *f.* 124r, the page meant to face a Crucifixion, a lion-shaped beast, its body filled with interlacing, is used as a large initial T and is shown accompanied by an intricate knot of snakes (pls. 47, 122). In this case it is not an allusion to St Mark, but again the symbol of the Resurrection, closely associated with the death of Christ. On the same page, however, there is another dragon head and a dragon tail which form the two ends of a frame. Are they purely ornamental and have we at last found a beast with no symbolic meaning? The same question arises when we come to the little lion-like creatures which prance so proudly in the intervals of the text: do they mean something, or are they just the liberated version of the animal-interlace with feline head? And are they lions, or at least the painter's notion of lions? Sometimes they seem to assume more familiar shapes: the cat gathered up on its haunches, watching a mouse-hole, or an emaciated cat seen from above, lying on the floor and busily licking its back (pl. 118, 83). Imperceptibly, we have come down from the dizzy heights of symbol and mystery to the most familiar of everyday realities, from transcendental theology to genre scenes. But caution is still necessary. These cats and kittens in the Chi-Rho page (pl. 107, bottom) are not engaged in a homely comedy. Whatever their exact meaning, they are gathered around a cross-bearing disc which brings them into line with the other symbols on the page.

Then we come to the interlace where two or more ribbon-like animals are combined in a regular pattern. Some of them have feline and some canine heads. These animated grilles already have a long tradition in Insular interlace. In the Book of Durrow, MS A. II. 17 at Durham and the manuscript in Cologne Cathedral, the animals are conventional, borrowed probably from stylized animals on metalwork. From the moment the manuscript painters adopted them, they attain a more animated and often more life-like appearance. Some-times they are combined with reminiscences of the animals which surround early Christian representations of the Foun-tain or the Tree of Life;[105] this must be the source for birds and quadrupeds woven together. In the Lichfield and Lindis-farne Gospels they cover large surfaces and in later manu-scripts they are found everywhere. But in the Book of Kells they are often intricate to the point of being baffling, and the animals composing the pattern can be disconcertingly protean. The page of the eight circles, for example, has combinations of quadrupeds and birds where some of the heads are inter-changeable (*f.* 33r: pls. 27, 108). In the four compartments and the panels of the border some of the ribbon-like bodies, coloured bright yellow, make a regular pattern amongst the

*Fig. 61 Spirals. Above: Turin, University Library, MS O.IV.20, detail. Below: Lichfield Cathedral, Lichfield Gospels, detail*

105. See Henry, *Irish Art I*, fig. 24.

*Fig. 62 Pictish engraved stone, Easterton, Roseisle (Elgin)*

Resurrection.[106] This is their meaning here, where they act as a kind of heraldic emblem of Christ, and their connection with eternal life is underlined by the presence of the little cross-marked discs on their shoulders. Where ambiguity arises is where they are shown again in the picture of 'the Lord' at the end of the genealogy of St Luke (f. 202r: pls. 67, 109, top). The panel shows two birds combined according to all the principles of animal interlace. They are most probably the two peacocks again, but this time submitted to the principles of ornament. From this to a panel of bird ornament inserted in a frame or the design of a monumental letter there is only one step, and how are we to know how much of its original meaning the motif may still carry?

There is another bird which looms large in the paintings of the Book: the eagle, symbol of St John, symbol also of Christ in heaven, and in fact a common emblem of God in early Christian art. It is found of course in all three four-symbols pages. It is a gorgeous bird in most cases, drawn with rich curves and bristling feathers (pls. 20, 50, 91, 92). It also appears frequently in the text, flying, opening its wings, flapping them (pl. 119). Generally it retains all the majesty of the symbolic eagle. But occasionally it comes curiously near in appearance to the barnacle goose, a familiar companion of the inhabitants of the Irish and Scottish coasts and islands (pl. 119, top). There again we land unobtrusively in everyday reality. This same confusion of appearance is found on some Pictish slabs (fig. 62). And various other aspects of that same bird combine with quadrupeds and snakes to make initials in the text (pl. 123). Other birds, even if they have a meaning connected with the text, such as the cock and hens (pl. 120, top), give us a glimpse of the farmyard which was no doubt attached to the monastery.

The animals which perhaps lend themselves most readily to interlacing are snakes; the Book teems with them. The snake can be a symbol of evil, a memory of the Fall of our first parents, but it can also be a symbol of eternity, or of resurrection, because it sheds its skin and comes out of it alive.[107] I am inclined to think that if it has a meaning in the pages of the Book it must be the latter, because of the confidence with which the painters spread whole patterns of snakes in the most conspicuous parts of the pages. They are in fact extraordinary beasts, as much figments of the painter's imagination as the lions of which he had probably never seen a live example. They are generally seen from above and have a large snout on both sides of which the eyes are inserted in oval or pear-shaped frames ending in long threads. The tail is crescent-shaped, triangular or sometimes three-pointed. Snakes of this type, or very similar ones, were used in the decoration of Irish metalwork.[108] There are some on the Tara brooch (fig. 64), and they form the essential motif of one side of the bronze objects in St Germain-en-Laye Museum. But they are a novelty in manuscripts. While their shape comes from metalwork, their widespread use was perhaps suggested by books like the Sacramentary of Gellone or the Amiens Psalter which are both full of snakes, though of a different type (figs. 63, 69).

maze of thin, duller lines (pl. 113). This tendency to give a definite rhythm to animal-interlace panels is very pronounced throughout the Book. In the frame of the portrait of Christ (f. 32v: pl. 26) the coiled bodies of the animals tend to give the illusion of a scroll of foliage. Elsewhere two bodies form an X pattern, the simplest arrangement of all (f. 255r: pl. 117), or several draw an elaborate knot (f. 29r: pl. 104).

These quadrupeds may combine with birds or birds may be used separately in the decoration of the Book. They are used in profusion already in the Lichfield and Lindisfarne Gospels, either alone (Chi-Rho of Lichfield) or interwoven with quadrupeds (carpet-pages of Lichfield and Lindisfarne). But in the Book of Kells they have close relations which are not purely ornamental and as it was in the case of the lion-dragon-cat which we have just examined, the gradation from symbol to decorative motif is often very subtle.

Let us first look at the two peacocks in the portrait of Christ page (f. 32v: pl. 26). These have been drawn with great care, even with a curiously realistic indication of the slight swelling at the base of the peacock's neck. Their function as emblems of Christ is well established. Two peacocks flanking a cross, a chalice or a fountain, their feet often entangled in vine scrolls (fig. 74), appear frequently in mosaics, sarcophagi and manuscript pages (fig. 34) during the first ten centuries of Christian art. As legend had it that the peacock's flesh did not putrefy, they were a symbol of the

---

106. H. Lother, *Der Pfau in der Altchristlichen Kunst*, Leipzig, 1929. Cf. St Augustine, *City of God : Quis enim nisi Deus dedit carni pavonis mortui ne putresceret?* (For who but God has ordained that the flesh of the peacock shall not corrupt in death?)

107. The Brazen Serpent is of course a symbol of Christ: see Réau, *Iconographie*, vol. II, 2, pp. 98–99.

108. The snake-like creatures on the Benty Grange enamelled disc and in an initial of Durham MS A.II.10 are of a different type, being shown with head in profile: see Henry, *Irish Art I*, fig. 20.

Fig. 63 *Amiens, Municipal Library, MS 18, initial*

A series of typical examples of their antics is to be found on *f.* 130r (pl. 51), the Introductory page of St Mark's Gospel. In one place, the centre of the pattern is formed by four heads giving the illusion of a sort of marigold (pl. 105). At the top, two heads and two tails combine to form the centre of the knot, and in the bold pattern at the bottom of the letters the opposition of two S-shaped yellow snakes with some blue ones makes the design. The serpent also appears separately and the painters have found its easy disposition to curves a great boon in framing displaced words (*f.* 337r: pl. 125) or stray letters (*f.* 52v: pl. 120).

The fish is another creature found frequently in the decoration of the Book. It is mostly used as the abbreviation sign over the *nomina sacra* – D\overline{nus}, D\overline{s}, Ih\overline{s} (*f.* 179v: pl. 116) – but it is found also occasionally as an ornament of the text where it is depicted carefully and minutely and in as lifelike a way as possible (*f.* 243v: pl. 119). It is, of course, an early Christian symbol whose popularity is based on the fact that its Greek name is an anagram of the name of Christ.

Other animals which remain independent of the ornament and do not seem to have any definite meaning add a few amusing items to the repertory of direct observation: a goat walking between the lines, a moth caught in the curve of a letter, etc. The wolf walking so purposefully across *f.* 76v (pl. 36) has been shown to have a close relationship with a similar figure engraved on a Scottish slab.[109]

The use of *plant ornament* is one of the characteristic features of the Book of Kells and one which makes it stand apart from the main group of Insular manuscripts. From this point of view, it takes its place nearer to the Barberini Gospels and the Prayer-book of Cerne than to any book with a more orthodox Insular decoration, though the foliage is of a different type, and the Book of Kells plant has sometimes more in common with that in the Amiens Psalter.

There are two different aspects of this foliage: it can consist of light, feathery sprays practically incorporated in the text, emerging from the end of a word, indicating a turn-in-the-path, or filling a gap (pls. 15, 18, 82, 97, 98). Such sprays are drawn quickly: a stem, two or three round red fruits, three or four dark green leaves, each done with one stroke of the brush. They are really an embellishment of the text, a frill to it; they seem to be equivalent to the little rosettes which replace

them on some pages as line-fillers. The other type of foliage is very different, though again it appears at first sight to be a purely decorative motif. On several pages it forms panels of vigorous scrolls encased in coloured frames. It fills the curve of the arch or the surface of a column on some of the canon-tables pages (*ff.* 2r, 4r: pls. 3, 7). In many cases the scrolls issue from a vase which is conical or, more often, cup-shaped, and rarely upright; it can be lying on its side or placed sideways in a corner of a frame, which seems to indicate that the important thing is the relationship between plant and cup, not the verisimilitude of a leafy bough whose stem is held by the vase or flower-pot.[110] In three cases, the meaning of the motif is made clear. In the page of the portrait of Christ (*f.* 32v: pl. 26), vines issuing from chalices are entangled around the peacocks' feet, establishing the link between Eucharist and Resurrection. On the Arrest page on both sides of the head of Christ are two vases with vines (*f.* 114r: pl. 45). Finally, at the end of the Lucan genealogy a vigorous double-stemmed vine shoots out of a chalice beside the two interlaced peacocks (*f.* 202r: pls. 67, 109, bottom).

This Kells vine is the oddest-looking botanical specimen. Like the lion and the snake, it is a product of the imagination of the painter who had probably never seen the real plant. His invention is however consistent and the type varies very little. It has a thick stem which sometimes enlarges into a sort of funnel at the junction with smaller stems (fig. 75). The leaves are long, pointed or rounded at the end, and there are generally three together. Fruit and flowers are scarce and are generally represented, as in the sprays in the text, by a little cluster of circles.

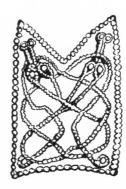

Fig. 64 *Dublin, National Museum, Tara Brooch, detail*

Occasionally, birds and animals feed from the fruit. The 'inhabited vine' is a common motif of early Christian art, an image of the Christians feeding on the Eucharist. It is found on such English metalwork as the Ormside cup and on a number of the English crosses. In Ireland it appears on the South Cross at Clonmacnois, on the side of the Cross of the Tower at Kells (fig. 65) and on the tenth-century Cross of Muiredach at Monasterboice. Among manuscripts, the Barberini Gospels present it clearly on the Chi-Rho page where it would have had its full symbolical meaning (fig. 31). In the Book of Kells it is found in its complete form only on a disc on *f.* 188r, where the vine is associated with birds and little quadrupeds (pls. 61, 115, top; fig. 65). There is also a spirited version of it in the line of decorative script in the title of the *Breves causae* of Luke where the letters play the part of quadrupeds (*f.* 19v: pl. 14; fig. 75). These few examples of inhabited vine are remarkable. The *Quoniam* motif includes false circles, the vegetable stem

109. Curle, *Chronology*, pl. XIX.
110. This treatment of vases is found in late Antique mosaics (fig. 65). It occurs also in the Barberini Gospel-book (fig. 66).

being drawn by compasses and giving the illusion of a full circle, when in fact the fourth quarter of the circle has not been drawn and the stem escapes unobtrusively to form new patterns (pl. 115; fig. 65). The Zacharias motif (pl. 103; fig. 75) has a freer arrangement of the stems. But in neither case does one find what Collingwood calls 'the tree-scroll' – the vine with a continuous central stem which is so frequent in Northumbrian crosses of the late eighth century (Croft, Jarrow, Hornby, Jedburgh).[111] This is the type of vine which is found, naturally enough, in the Barberini manuscript, probably Northumbrian

in origin (fig. 31). The three examples of inhabited vine on Irish crosses are devoid of the continuous central trunk, though the Kells cross has a half-hearted beginning of it (fig. 65). They all have a constant passing of the stems from one side to the other, forming irregular 'false-circles'. This is closer to the pattern on the mosaic in the Louvre (fig. 65) and may have been transmitted from the East by ivories or illuminations. Besides these false-circles patterns there are also in the borders of the Book of Kells simple scrolls of foliage with or without animals (ff. 2r, 4r, 8r, 129v, 285r; pls. 3, 7, 11, 50, 89).[112]

111. W. G. Collingwood, *Northumbrian Crosses*, London, 1927, figs. 96, 59, 71, 57.

112. F. Henry, *La sculpture irlandaise*, Paris, 1932, figs. 29, 78.

# THE PAINTERS

An abundantly decorated manuscript such as the Book of Kells raises several questions about those responsible for its decoration. The two chief ones concern the relationship between scribes and painters and the possibility that several painters were engaged in the execution of the large illustrations.

Let us examine the text decoration first. The ornament surrounding the genealogy in Matthew has never been finished and so can be a useful starting point. The scribe planned for the decoration to come and fitted his text into a smaller space than usual to allow for an ornamental frame around the three first pages. The double page 30v–31r (pls. 24–25) is the most readily intelligible. On folio 31r the scribe made the lozenge-shaped initial O of *Omnes* the centre of the decoration. Then he planned another lozenge, purely ornamental, in the corres-ponding place of folio 30v. For greater safety, and so that the scheme should not be forgotten – by him or somebody else – he drew both lozenges and applied some colour. He also wanted discs and half-discs for ornament, so he took his compasses and drew some circles. He also drew a frame, very lightly in ink with a ruler, using the guiding line which has the prickings for the lines of text as his outside contour and a second line directly framing the text as the inside one. On the right (*f.* 31r) this could hardly be more than a guide for the restricted text, though the intention of having a frame is already manifest. On 30v, things went somewhat further and two opposite corners are worked out in a delicate, incisive pen-drawing that is already coloured. On the top left hand corner, the heads of a lion and an eagle have been sketched in. On the right bottom corner the hind legs of the lion with claws sharply indicated are entangled with the feathery tail of an eagle. Here the pattern begins to take shape, possibly even the shape of two Evangelical symbols treated as an ornament. One cannot avoid the feeling that scribe and painter worked in close accord and that the man who traced these schematic indications was probably the scribe himself, but we do not know whether he intended to come back and complete them or whether he expected some-body else to do it. The same process is shown by an unfinished initial T on *f.* 64r (pl. 35) and an unfinished interlinear figure on *f.* 99v (pl. 40); the T has been traced in green paint, but additional ornaments and the black final drawing are missing; the figure lacks also the black lines which would define its shape with precision.

Was this always the case or were ordinary text pages treated differently? It was a common habit of medieval scribes to leave spaces available where decorated initials would be inserted later, and as in many cases they have not been filled the process can be seen very clearly. In the light of this, let us look at a few pages of the Book. Folio 91r (pl. 39) gives a good example of how the painter can follow the intentions of the scribe: each initial fits in well with the space allotted to it and fills it adequately. But what of 111r (pl. 43)? There, the scribe may have traced the heavy black outlines of the first five initials, leaving the painter to add colour embellishments to them. But the last one, made of an animal and bird, is probably all devised by the painter and it encroaches on the margin and on the writing space in all directions. Then, to introduce the sentences said by Christ, the painter added an eagle and a lion which had probably not been foreseen. Turning the pages of the Book one comes to the conclusion that this is the regular pro-cess, that the scribe left square or rectangular spaces which the painters used for irregular and most fancifully shaped initials.

Whether in some cases it was the scribe himself, who, the calligraphy of his page finished to his satisfaction, turned to his brushes and paint to enliven the page he had just written, is hard to decide. The only thing which might prove it would be a regular correspondence between a certain type of script and a certain style of initials. We have seen that there are at least three different hands in the Book. There is a possibility that Hand B may be associated with a certain type of initial with unusually large animals and wide coloured ribbons. This is the case with the initial of the *Breves causae* of John, so different from the spectacular headings of the other prefaces, with the large A in the beginning of the list of Hebrew names on folio 26r, and with the *Vespere autem* which marks the Resurrection in Matthew (*f.* 127v: pl. 48). But there are initials of this type in other parts of the Book which do not correspond with the characteristic of Hand B, such as the initial of the *Pater* in St Matthew's Gospel (*f.* 45r: pl. 31). So the question remains open. That scribes were also painters is proved by the example of Mac Regol who describes himself as having painted his book (*depincxit*) and as being its scribe (*scriptor*). Bruce-Mitford thinks that it can be proved that Eadfrith was the painter as well as the scribe of the Book of Lindisfarne. So this would be no unusual case. The scribe of Hand B may have used his own style of initials in the texts which he wrote and may also have added initials in spaces left blank by other scribes.

In one place, however, one may wonder what happened: the reverse of the *Quoniam* (*f.* 188r: pl. 61), the Introductory page of St Luke (*f.* 188v: pl. 62) seems to be written by Hand B in an imitation of the script used in that part of the Book, probably by Hand C. The text proper of St Luke, after the short prologue, starts with a very splendid initial of the very type associated with Hand B. Does that mean that the scribe-painter was given the *Quoniam* to paint and went on, writing the text on the back and adding one of his own characteristic initials? As the *Quoniam* does not fit in at all with the other Introductory pages, one is tempted to assume that it may be the work of the scribe-painter B, an assumption which must remain hypothetical.

Before leaving the initials let us take an overall view of them. What seems remarkable is their homogeneity. True, they can be divided into a number of categories. Apart from those which are based on the tracery of a black line and the more fanciful ribbon-initials, there are some with animals only, some formed in irregular patterns, and others which are built to a strict form around square panels of interlacing. There are also those which end with heads, human or animal. But all of these types are scattered through the whole Book, in a repertory which does not change widely for any part.

Many painters probably worked on these initials and interlinear decorations, but one personality seems to stand out, that of the man who added between the lines and around the 'turns' a host of little wandering animals. He shows a great sense of observation and occasionally a keen sense of humour. He works more freely than the other painters, introducing beside their solemn compositions a more fanciful note and occasionally using details of everyday life.

What about the painting of the full-page illuminations? These were in many cases done on single leaves which could be distributed to the painters to be done separately and then inserted in the Book at binding. This is probably one reason why most of them – portraits, four-symbols pages, carpet-page – have blank reverses. The illustrations in the text – the Arrest (*f.* 114r: pl. 45) and the Temptation (*f.* 203r: pl. 69) – were no doubt painted after the scribe had finished his work as there was writing on the back of them. The page which had been earmarked for a Crucifixion and left blank is sufficient proof of it.

That these large pages are not all from the same hand is fairly obvious. Returning to a detailed study of the Book after an interval of many years, and after its pages had been flattened prior to rebinding, which might have changed their character somewhat, I was quite prepared to find that what I had proposed earlier as the work of the three chief painters of the Book had lost some of the clear evidence which it seemed to present in the past.[113] In fact, I was surprised to see how much of my earlier suggestions still stood and I am proposing roughly the same distribution of styles as before.

But even if some personalities can be detected, it is essential to remember that the Book is the work of a whole scriptorium working together and that several pages may be due to colla-boration between painters of uneven gifts. It is also noteworthy that no single painter is responsible for all the illuminations of one Gospel. They all work simultaneously, thanks to the fact that the single leaves can be distributed right and left and painted while the text is being written. There may even have been a deliberate effort to use the work of the various painters in rotation, so that the different styles would be more or less evenly spread through the Book.

One of the painters, whom I earlier called the 'Gold-smith', because of the way in which his compositions try to suggest metalwork by their constant use of golden yellow and silvery blue and the clear-cut incisiveness of his incredibly intricate patterns, seems to have painted the Introductory pages of the Gospels, except that of St Luke, the page of the eight circles and the Chi-Rho (pls. 23, 51, 95, 27, 29). I would be inclined also to see his hand in the upper part of folio 5r (pl. 9) in the canon-tables. He is certainly the greatest draughtsman in the Book, working in a tradition of graphism which connects the Lichfield Gospels to the Book of Armagh. He uses a slightly archaic repertoire where the spiral holds pride of place and he never uses foliage decoration, which is an intrusion in the most traditional Insular work. On the other hand, he uses snakes a good deal, which are also unusual in these manuscripts.

That he did three of the Introductory pages whose reverse is always a page of text establishes a close link between him and the scribe of Hand C, though I would hesitate to say that they were one and the same man. But it is possible that their collaboration led the Goldsmith to take part in some of the text decoration.

The 'Illustrator' is a very different person. Not for him the arachnean intricacies of spirals and interlace. His interest is essentially in figures, weird and immobile but impressive in the extreme. He painted the Temptation (pl. 68), the Arrest (pl. 45) and also the Virgin and Child (pl. 10) and perhaps the four-symbols page of St John (pl. 92). He may have worked at the *Nativitas* page (pl. 11) but, if so, he must have done it in collaboration, as some of the details are difficult to reconcile with his impatience of minutiae. He was fond of violent, almost aggressive colours and used washes of purple and green in semi-transparent layers to great effect. He used vegetable ornament freely. Judging by the way in which he breaks the columns on both sides of the Arrest, he seems insensitive to architecture, though when it comes to describing a type of building he knew, as he did with the Temple, assimilated by him with some important local church, he shows a vigorous grasp of structure. He may have worked on some of the canon-tables, but probably in collaboration.

The 'Portrait Painter' is the author of the portrait of Christ (pl. 26) and of the portraits of the Evangelists (pls. 22, 94). Less of a visionary than the Illustrator, slightly matter-of-fact, he nonetheless produced in the St John page (pl. 94) a very arresting composition. He may well be the author of the four-symbols page in St Matthew's Gospel (pl. 20).

So a great number of hands have probably collaborated in producing a fairly coherent and harmonious decoration. Like the scribes, the painters belonged to a scriptorium where there were no watertight compartments and there was sufficient give and take to produce a common flavour in the work, whatever the individual tendencies of the artists.

---

113. *Irish Art in the early Christian Period*, London, 1940, pp. 144 ff., repeated without much change in *Irish Art II*, pp. 73 ff.

# CONCLUSION

From our review of its various aspects, the Book of Kells stands out as an unusual manuscript not only for the wealth of its decoration, but for the multiplicity of contacts it reveals.

There can be no doubt that it belongs to the group of Insular manuscripts and in many ways seems one of its most typical examples. It shows a variety of connections with several of them in particular, as well as a general accord with the metalwork and the carvings which form their background. In its script and text it is closely linked with the most Irish of the Insular manuscripts, though it has affinities also with others. Some of the various hands which can be detected in its script have connections with the Book of Mac Regol and the Book of Armagh, both signed by Irish scribes. But another has close similarities to the Lichfield Gospels and Durham MS A.II.17, whose origin is not as definite. Its main text is a typical example of the mixed Irish version of the Gospels. It agrees with the Book of Durrow and the Book of Armagh in the choice of the prefaces and with the Book of Durrow in their erratic order. Its range of colours links it with the Lindisfarne and Lichfield Gospels, though it is nearer to the latter in its use of superimposed layers of colours and transparent glazes.

It agrees with the whole group of Insular manuscripts in the general trend of its decoration, in the overpowering predominance of ornament absorbing into its regular compositions even some elements of symbolism and representation. Most of its decorative motifs are not only typically Insular, but appear at a stage of especially rich and probably late development. But when it is analysed closely, it is found to contain one intruding element, namely foliage patterns. The continuous and elaborate decoration of the text is also an unusual feature.

In the same way, though the tendency to reduce figures to geometrical or decorative patterns is very strong in the Book – and this is a definite characteristic of the most thoroughly Insular figure representation – the very abundance of these figure representations is unusual for an Insular manuscript. So, depending on the angle from which it is considered, the Book appears both as the most thoroughly Insular of all Insular manuscripts and as the least representative of the group.

These two anomalies – the abundance of figured pages and use of foliage ornament on the one hand and the elaborate decoration of the text on the other – are evidence of various affinities either with manuscripts slightly peripheric to the Insular group or with models from far away.

Let us consider first the extensive use of full-page illustrations. The question of the source of inspiration of these pictures has already been raised. Very little in that line is likely to have been completely invented by the painters of the Book of Kells. That they adapted, transformed, magnified or misunderstood their models is obvious. But models they had. What they were and where they came from is one of the most vexed and fascinating questions concerning the Book and various answers have been given to it, ranging from that of Friend who saw the exemplar of the Book in one of the early Carolingian manuscripts,[114] to that proposed recently by Martin Werner who finds in some pages of the Book a reflection of some lost Coptic manuscripts.[115]

The possibility of a link between Insular manuscripts and the art of Christian Egypt has often preoccupied scholars[116] and is made especially attractive by the extraordinary similarity of the Book of Durrow to Coptic manuscripts, in colour, in the lay-out of some pages and in the use of some patterns, chiefly interlacings.[117] An earlier Irish manuscript, the Orosius of Bobbio, has a page similar to some Coptic bindings.[118] But so far the difficulty had been that no decorated Coptic manuscript earlier than the ninth century seemed to have survived, so that all arguments were based on these late manuscripts. The publication by H. Bober of the Glazier Codex,[119] a Coptic manuscript of much earlier date (c. 400) including some coloured interlace, has made it possible to assume that there were in fact Coptic decorated manuscripts earlier than the Book of Durrow which could have been partly its models. That some of them also had figure illuminations similar to those found in ninth- and tenth-century preserved examples can now be accepted more readily.

An explanation of how these contacts took place is also now forthcoming, as traces of an extensive trade between the Near East and the coasts of Ireland, Scotland and England have been found in quantity in the last decades.[120] The jars

---

114. Friend, *Canon Tables*.

115. Werner, *Madonna and Child*.

116. P. Meyer in *E.Q.C. Durm.*, p. 166 and *E.Q.C. Cenan.*; N. Åberg, *The Occident and the Orient in the Art of the Seventh Century*, vol. I, Stockholm, 1943; Wessel, *Coptic Art*, pp. 232–3; *contra*: J. Raftery, in *J.R.S.A.I.*, 1965, pp. 193 ff.

117. M. Cramer, *Koptische Buchmalerei*, Recklinghausen, 1964.

118. F. Henry, 'Les origines de la miniature irlandaise', *Gazette des Beaux-Arts*, 1950, pp. 5 ff. (figs. 4 and 6).

119. H. Bober, 'On the Illumination of the Glazier Codex', *Homage to a Bookman*, Berlin, 1967, pp. 31 ff.

120. C. A. Ralegh Radford, 'Imported Pottery at Tintagel, Cornwall', *Dark Age Britain*, London, 1956, pp. 59 ff.; C. Thomas, 'Imported Pottery in Dark Age Western Britain', *Medieval Archaeology*, 1959, pp. 89 ff.

which were the chief article of exportation from the East were often stamped with crosses and may have supplied the liturgical needs of the Western Churches in wine and oil. The ruins of some Coptic monasteries have produced fragments of the same type of pottery, which is also represented from Constantinople. This opens up a vast perspective of comings and goings between the Near East and the islands of the West, at a time when the Christian communities in these islands were to a great extent isolated from the Continent by the barrier of pagan England. Boats being available, it is not impossible that some Insular monks repeated for their own instruction the journey made a little earlier by Cassian who went from the south of Gaul to visit the monasteries of Egypt, the inspiration of all early monasteries. Books may well have been brought back from such journeys and used as models by the Insular scriptoria. This would explain, to a certain extent, the style of decoration of the Bobbio Orosius, Durham MS A. II. 10, the Book of Durrow, and the *Collectio Canonum* of Cologne.[121]

These contacts, however, occur in the fifth, sixth and perhaps early seventh centuries. But then the trade seems to stop, probably because of the arrival of the Arabs on the coasts of the Mediterranean. At the same time, England was becoming Christian, converted in the north by Irish missionaries from Iona, and in the south by missions from Rome. So the Insular Churches which had had only rare contacts with the Continent found it all suddenly open before them. From that time on, the chief links were with Italy, especially with Rome, and these had considerable artistic consequences.

For Ireland, the contacts with the Continent occurred early. St Columbanus left probably directly from Scotland, in the late sixth century and eventually founded Bobbio in northern Italy at a time when paganism was only beginning to yield in England. Bobbio kept in close contact with Bangor in Ireland, where St Columbanus had been a monk. Travellers must have come and gone, bringing back gifts, and that would explain the fact that in a description of the church of Kildare written in the mid seventh century it is said to have a decoration of pictures (*decorata pictis tabulis*).[122] About thirty years later, Benedict Biscop brought back from Rome pictures which hung in the church at Wearmouth, among them images of the Virgin and of the Apostles.[123] Then the contact became intensified in Jarrow-Wearmouth at the time when the Codex Amiatinus was written and decorated with imitations of imported illuminations.

However, of what came from Italy a good deal was of Greek origin or was influenced by Byzantine models. In the seventh and eighth century Rome was full of Oriental painters and probably of Oriental manuscripts, either through the influence of men of Oriental origin, such as Pope John VII, or as a consequence of the Iconoclastic quarrel which caused a number of Byzantine artists, deprived of employment and possibly in danger, to drift to the West and work there. That Insular painters had in their hands manuscripts in Greek is shown by the imitation Greek inscriptions which accompany the Lindisfarne Evangelist portraits. Sometimes there is no more than an echo of the original Greek, as in some of the text accompanying the Ascension in the Turin Gospel-book (fig. 19).

So, after the seventh century, the likelihood of an overpowering Coptic influence becomes less. There must have been Coptic manuscripts among those imported, just as there may have been Syriac or Armenian ones, but the main bulk was probably Byzantine. Of the Syriac and Coptic ones, the symbols on *f*. 11 are probably witnesses, as a text written from right to left would be accompanied by a set of symbols made to be read from the right. In fact it is hardly likely that any one model was followed exactly or constantly. Models seem to have been of an extreme diversity. We saw that a few of the animal symbols in the Book are shown with human hands, while most of the others are in full animal shape. This points to at least two different sources of inspiration for this motif alone.

The use of foliage ornament and the decoration of the text which are characteristic of the Book of Kells are also features of the Book of Cerne and the Barberini Gospel-book, both of which are written in Anglo-Saxon script and have decoration including a constant use of sprightly little animals of pure English style. These two manuscripts and the Leningrad Gospels which are closely akin to them have been ascribed to various parts of England, though Lindisfarne is their most likely place of origin. The Barberini manuscript is signed by Uigbald or Huigbald, who wrote probably the greatest part of it. This name, which is not very common, is that of the abbot of Lindisfarne who governed the monastery from 760 to 803 and was a friend of Alcuin. He was abbot in 793 when Lindisfarne was wrecked by the Vikings, and to this may be due, perhaps, some of the very incoherent aspects of the decoration of the book. The Book of Cerne comes from the abbey of Cerne in Dorset, but it has an acrostic and some headings which refer it to Eadeluald Episcopus. Edmond Bishop has suggested that the 'Book of Aethelwald' was only the model copied by the scribe, and that this Aethelwald was the bishop of Lindisfarne who governed the monastery from 721 to 740.[124] It is a sort of early Book of Hours and includes a number of prayers showing definite Irish affinities. There is no historical reason for linking the Leningrad Gospels with Lindisfarne, except its similarity with the two other manuscripts.[125] The Maeseyck fragment might also belong to this milieu, or to York, as Nordenfalk has suggested, but not in the time of Wilfrid. The capitals of the arch framing the Evangelist (fig. 39) can be paralleled on late eighth-century carved stones such as the Castor carvings,[126] and the figure itself has too much in common with the Evangelists in the Barberini Gospel-book not to be roughly contemporary with them. As a working hypothesis, we shall accept the fact that they all emanate from Lindisfarne or its neighbourhood in the late eighth century.

The letters of Alcuin go a long way to define the artistic

*Fig. 66 Vatican Library, MS Barberini Lat. 570, foliage*

121. The connections with Visigothic Spain often stressed recently and perhaps overestimated would date from the same period; see J. N. Hillgarth, 'Visigothic Spain and Early Christian Ireland', *P.R.I.A.*, 1962 (C), pp. 167 ff., and Werkmeister, in the same volume.

122. See Bieler, *Ireland*, p. 28; Henry, *Irish Art I*, p. 89.

123. See above, n. 63.

124. Dom A. B. Kuypers, O.S.B., *The Prayer-Book of Aedeluald the Bishop, commonly called the Book of Cerne*, Cambridge, 1902; E. Bishop,

*Liturgica Historica*, Oxford, 1918; D. N. Dumville, 'Biblical Apocrypha and the Early Irish', *P.R.I.A.*, 1973 (C), pp. 299 ff. (p. 321). On these manuscripts see: Henry, *Irish Art*, II, pp. 60 ff.

125. It has some textual relationship with the Book of Lindisfarne and the Codex Amiatinus: see D. Wright in *Art Bulletin*, 1961, pp. 151-52, n. 50 (review of *The Relics of St Cuthbert*).

126. Kendrick, *Anglo-Saxon Art*, pl. LXIX.

atmosphere of this milieu which one would expect at first sight to have become thoroughly English and perhaps to have lost contact with the Insular style. It seems, on the contrary, that Irishmen had drifted into it again.[127] Alcuin had an Irish master, Colgu, probably at York, and when he went to the Continent to work for Charlemagne took with him a certain Joseph, who was an Irish pupil of Colgu. There is also a mention in a contemporary poem[128] of an Irish painter, Ultán, active at that time in a monastery depending on Lindisfarne. And, of course, painters working on the island had under their eyes the Book of Lindisfarne itself from which they could draw inspiration. The mixture of some very English features, such as the treatment of the animals, with Insular ones would be readily explicable in such surroundings.

But the relationship of these manuscripts with the Book of Kells is not so easy to establish. They obviously point to a close contact between Lindisfarne and the place of origin of the Book of Kells. At the same time they belong to a different world. Rather than manifesting an influence one way or the other they seem to be witnesses to a common background shared with Kells.

In fact their relationship with Kells is nearly the same as that of the two Canterbury manuscripts, the Codex Aureus of Stockholm[129] and the Cotton Psalter Vespasian A.I. In the use of gold and silver and of purple-dyed parchment the Stockholm Gospels are completely alien to Kells; in the type of most of their animals both manuscripts are clearly English; but their spiral-patterns are Insular and some of the canon-tables of the Gospels are very close to those of the Book of Kells. Add to that the fact that one of the Kells scribes knows about the use of various colours of ink, and you have a relationship which is parallel to that between Kells and the Lindisfarne group. The Book of Kells is no more likely to have been written in Lindisfarne than in Canterbury. In both cases there are exchanges, penetration of Insular patterns on the one hand and novelties on the other. In Canterbury, the novelties can be traced to the presence of a Byzantine manuscript. For the Lindisfarne group and Kells the case is slightly different, and though Byzantine books are probably the ultimate source of new experiments, these experiments were probably first made on the Continent.

A series of manuscripts from the north of France, which we have already mentioned, seems to throw some light on the way in which new methods were elaborated. Several of them come from the neighbourhood of Amiens, from Corbie especially. Near Corbie and in close contact with it was an old Irish foundation, Perrona Scottorum, now Péronne, which seems to have been governed by Irish abbots until its destruction by the Vikings in 880. Traube has shown the close relations which existed between Corbie, Centula (St Riquier) and Péronne on the one hand and English and Irish monasteries on the other.[130] Péronne owned important Irish texts relating to St Patrick;[131] all three monasteries also possessed English manuscripts. They were the normal port of call of Insular travellers arriving on the Continent. Alcuin may have come that way, as we see from his letters that he knew the abbots of Corbie and of Centula.

This was a curious artistic and intellectual milieu whose Byzantine connections are stressed by the presence of a Greek, George, in the see of Amiens during the last thirty years of the eighth century. He had been bishop of Ostia before coming to the court of Pepin and then of his son Charlemagne. As a papal legate he made a journey to England. He wrote a Latin translation of the Greek Alexandrian World Chronicle of which a copy was made in Corbie. Corbie had other contacts with Byzantinizing Italy: King Desiderius of the Lombards, who had erected the Tempietto of Cividale, died in the monastery.

The chief manuscripts connected with this group of monasteries are the Amiens Psalter (Amiens, Municipal Library, MS 18) dating from around 800,[132] and, of a slightly later date, the manuscript from the monastery of Sainte Croix in the Municipal Library of Poitiers, the manuscripts in Corbie script in the Cathedral of Essen, and probably the Psalter in Stuttgart (figs. 42, 48). For a long time they attracted little attention, partly perhaps because of their unusual character and the way in which they did not conform to the norm of either Merovingian or Carolingian art. But already in 1940 G. L. Micheli pointed out the links between the Amiens Psalter and Insular art.[133] Jean Porcher gave particular attention to the whole group in his last years,[134] and stressed the way in which Insular and Byzantine traits are found in them. The ambivalent character of these contacts is very striking, especially in the Amiens Psalter, which has such strong elements of Insular decoration that Porcher went so far as to write that its painter 'came from the British Isles or had been trained there'.[135] He certainly uses motifs of Insular decoration, chiefly interlace and animal interlace. But he involves them in compositions which are new to Insular art, some of which appear also in the Book of Kells (figs. 67, 68). This gives a picture of exchanges, of a milieu where novel formulas were being evolved. It can be completed by adding to the group of manuscripts from the region of Amiens the Sacramentary of Gellone,[136] of similar date, which may come from the convent of Chelles near Paris, which was founded like Corbie by St Bathild and may have kept some connection with it. The pages of the Sacramentary have brilliantly coloured initials of an extraordinary variety, which, like those of the Amiens Psalter, have in many cases some subtle bearing

127. Henry, *Irish Art*, II, pp. 27 ff.: W. Wattenbach and X. Duemmler, *Monumenta Alcuiniana*, Berlin, 1873.

128. *Symeonis Monachi Opera Omnia*, ed. Th. Arnold, I, London, 1882, pp. 265 ff. and 273 ff.

129. C. Nordenfalk, 'A Note on the Stockholm Codex Aureus', *Nordisk Tidskrift för Bok och Biblioteksväsen*, 1952, oo. 145 ff.

130. L. Traube, 'Perrona Scottorum', *Sitzberichte der Bayerische Akademie*, Munich, 1900.

131. Bieler, *Ireland*, p. 99.

132. Some other manuscripts have a few initials in the same style: Amiens MS 7 (a Bible), Paris, Lat. 4884 (the translation of the Alexandrian Chronicle).

133. Micheli, *Enluminure*, pp. 86–87.

134. Hubert-Porcher-Volbach, p. 202.

135. J. Porcher, 'L'Evangéliaire de Charlemagne et le Psautier d'Amiens', *Revue des Arts*, 1957, pp. 51 ff., and 'Aux origines de la lettre ornée', *Mélanges Tisserand*, Biblioteca Vaticana, 1964; see also n. 132, above.

136. Cf. Nordenfalk: 'The Gellone Sacramentary is a kind of Merovingian counterpart of the Book of Kells', in Grabar and Nordenfalk, *Painting*, p. 134. See B. Tessèdre, *Le Sacramentaire de Gellone*, 1959; and the Turnhout publication: *Sacramentarium Gellonense, cura et studio A. Dumas* (Corpus Christianarum, tomus CLIX).

*Fig. 67 Book of Kells, initial (f. 283r)*

on the text they introduce (figs. 50, 69). Here again there are traces of Insular influence in the use of some patterns, and the initials are made of human and animal figures bent to the shape of the letters (fig. 69). That there is a Byzantine impulse at the root of all this is shown by some characteristic details which can only be direct borrowings from a Byzantine model. One of them is the use of human arms in initials. In the Sacramentary they are flung sideways with a flippant casualness (fig. 69). In the Amiens Psalter the Byzantine blessing hand is imitated more faithfully (fig. 70). In the Book of Kells, a very prominent pointing hand (*f.* 58v: pl. 124) has probably the same origin. The use of a Greek inscription above the head of Christ in the Poitiers manuscript points in the same direction (fig. 48). So Byzantine models probably fostered the development of manuscripts enlivened by a great number of varied and animated initials. One may assume that they are also the origin of the decoration in the text and of the extensive use of foliage as an ornament. These models must have circulated in scriptoria of northern France where borrowings from them were elaborated, perhaps partly by wandering Insular scribes, and then transmitted by them to their monasteries.[137]

One aspect of the Book of Kells is very strange and if studied in more detail might throw some light on its background: the complex nature of its iconography. It certainly has an undercurrent of early Christian thought. The representation of God, generally the Second Person of the Trinity, as a partly hidden or only partly described figure goes back to images like the Crucifixion with a half-length figure of Christ above the cross which is found on early Christian ampullae, or to the Transfiguration in Sant' Apollinare in Classe in Ravenna with the cross substituted for Christ. Were particular models followed here, or did a local development of thought bring about the creation of these strange images? But on the other hand, some aspects of the iconography of the Book of Kells are in the vanguard of pictorial representations of the time. The Book has the earliest representation in a Western manuscript of the Virgin and Child; it has perhaps the earliest representations of the Temptation of Christ, of the Tree of Jesse and of the lion as symbol of Resurrection. It competes here with Carolingian manuscripts with which it is contemporary and with which its connections are so elusive.[138]

It remains now to deal with the vexed question of the date of the Book and of the place where it was written and decorated. Various dates have been proposed for it since the Book has attracted the attention of scholars. Discarding the fantastically early dates proposed in a first wave of enthusiasm, most of the hypotheses centre on a mid eighth-century date or one around 800. From the comparisons we have had to make, which are practically all with works of the late eighth or early ninth century, it seems that the Book belongs to a period roughly between 790 and 820 or 830.

If we now try to guess at its place of origin – and we can do no more than guess – it is necessary to remember the various connections of script, text and decoration, and also to form some idea of the milieu which could foster such a work. In dealing with the iconography, we have had to insist on its extreme subtlety, on its almost esoteric character. A monastery capable of evolving such a complex and sometimes abstruse imagery must have had a long tradition of intellectual speculation. It must also have been endowed with a whole library of imported books, which at that time accumulated only slowly. And it must have been rich, by the standards of the time,[139] to

*Fig. 68 Amiens, Municipal Library, MS 18, initial*

---

137. For the origin of the zoomorphic initial see C. Nordenfalk, *Die Spätantiken Zierbuchstaben*, Stockholm, 1970. Meyer Shapiro seems to assume that it originated in Italy and spread from there to East and West (M. Shapiro, 'The Florence Dietissaron', *Art Bull.*, LV, 4, pp. 494 ff.). His argument is open to discussion like all arguments based on 'the earliest *dated* manuscript' to have a certain feature. Anyway, the bishop of Amiens, who had lived in Italy, could have brought an assorted collection of manuscripts with him.

138. The whole problem of the relationship of the Book of Kells and the earliest Carolingian manuscripts needs fresh investigation. Friend's

theory fails to be convincing and hardly fits with the chronological data. Nonetheless, there are striking similarities.

139. See K. Hughes, 'The Distribution of Irish Scriptoria and Centres of Learning from 730 to 1111', *Studies in the Early British Church*, Cambridge, 1958. See in: Henry, *Irish Art III*, pp. 34–35, the 'circuit' made by Flathbertach O'Brolchain, abbot of Derry and at that time head of the Columban monasteries, to collect the various tributes he was entitled to in order to rebuild the church of Derry; he visited affiliated monasteries as far as Leinster and Ossory.

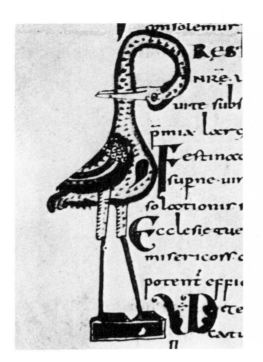

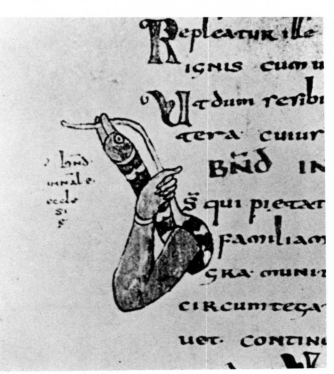

Fig. 69 Paris, National Library, MS Lat. 12048 (Sacramentary of Gellone), initials

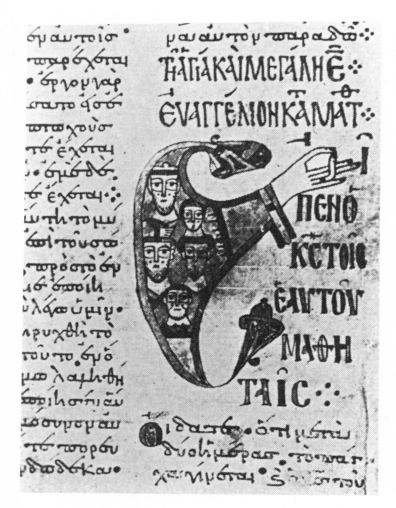

*Fig. 70 Vatican Library, MS Gr. 2138, initial; Amiens, Municipal Library, MS 18, initial*

indulge in the luxury of decorating its altar with a book absorbing the activities of perhaps a dozen elaborately trained scribes and illuminators for several decades. The Book's connections, as we have seen, are with Ireland, with the Iona crosses, occasionally with the Pictish art of Scotland, with some manuscripts which are probably from Lindisfarne, with manuscripts from Canterbury and with manuscripts originating from monasteries connected with an Irish foundation on the Continent. I must say that in view of all this the old hypothesis of Iona-Kells still appeals to me as the most convincing. There is no mention of the plunder of Kells by the Vikings until the end of the ninth century. When it was established, the monastery seems to have settled in an old stronghold which probably kept all attacks at bay for a long time. It is also likely that the monastery bought its peace by paying tribute to the Vikings. Anyhow, that long respite means that the Book could have been begun in Iona in the late eighth century and completed (though never absolutely finished) in the first quarter of the ninth century in Kells. There are enough parallels in carvings in both places to back this hypothesis. Crosses at Iona and the neighbouring Kildalton have representations of the Virgin and Child surrounded by angels which seem, as far as the wear of the stone allows one to

judge, to fit in with the Virgin and Child page in the Book (pl. 10, fig. 37). Carvings and miniature may all have been based on some icon owned by the monastery. In addition the type of complex spiral pattern (fig. 73) or snake-spiral arrangement found on these crosses fits in with elaborate pages of the Book like the Monogram (pl. 29) or some of the Introductory pages. It is striking that the Cross of the Tower of Kells, which probably belongs to the early ninth century, is the only one of the Irish high crosses to have the symbols of the Evangelists. It has, in fact, the whole Apocalyptic Vision (fig. 72). The carvings differ in this from the more elusive figurations in the Book, but it is understandable that the sculptor, having in view a less sophisticated audience, did not feel as inclined to subtlety as the painter who was working for a few theologically minded monks. In any case, the symbols are there, and they link the Cross and the Book. The Cross also has an inhabited vine built on the same principles as that on the *Quoniam* page of the Book (fig. 65).

Connections between Iona and Lindisfarne, originally its daughter-house, are only to be expected. In fact, in the late eighth century, the first stage of a journey from Iona to the Continent was no doubt the well-trodden and fairly easy road Iona–Melrose–Lindisfarne.[140] The link with Canterbury is

---

140. J. Brown seems to assume that the journey Lindisfarne-Iona was a long and difficult one, involving at the end 'a long sea journey'. It did not. Travellers used to cross from near Oban to Mull, a short and sheltered passage, then cross the island until they reached the narrow sound between Mull and Iona. There, they 'shouted' for a boat which came from Iona to

fetch them. There are innumerable references to this in Adamnan's *Life of St Columba*. Anyway, it is impossible to overestimate the capacity for travel of the Insular monks. On Melrose (Old Melrose) as a stop on the road from Lindisfarne to Iona, see Henry, *Irish Art I*, p. 34.

Fig. 71 Amiens, Municipal Library, MS 18, initials

*Fig. 72 Kells, Cross of the Tower, west side, Apocalyptic Vision*

less obvious, though a journey by land to the English port nearest to the Continent would almost automatically mean a stop in Canterbury. We may thus have in these connected manuscripts – Book of Kells, manuscripts from Lindisfarne, Canterbury manuscripts and books from the neighbourhood of Corbie – the milestones of the travels to and from the Continent of Insular scribes and scholars.

One would like to go further and to understand how the various stages of the work on the Book developed. But here, the number of clear data is very small. The parts written by Hand A, definitely archaic in style of script, can be attributed to Iona. This means *ff.* 1r and 7–19 of the preliminaries (pls. 1, 10–14), and most of the surviving part of the Gospel of St John. Could the Virgin and Child and the canon-tables

*Fig. 73 Iona, detail of stone cross*

be included too? Given the connections of the Virgin with a carving in Iona, it seems likely that it was painted there. The similarity between the Kells canon-tables and those of the Codex Aureus, ascribable to the mid eighth century, may mean that they belong also to that early phase of the work. But they may have been unfinished when the move to Kells took place. As it is difficult to connect them in style with the other decorated pages of the Book, they are possibly due to a team of painters who do not reappear in Kells. In this context, I have already mentioned that the Annals of Ulster record the death of Connachtach, 'eminent scribe and abbot of Ia' (Iona), in 802, the date of the first Viking attack on Iona.[141] He may have been Scribe A, whose hand does not reappear in other parts of the Book, and he may have devised the pro-gramme of its decoration. Why the Book should have been started from both ends we do not know, but it is not impossible that part of the text was lost in the plundering of the monastery. Whether the work of the Goldsmith, which is also fairly archaic in style, can be ascribed to this period is impossible to tell. All we can assume is that Scribe C worked in Kells. And if the Illustrator had painted the Virgin and Child (pl. 10) in Iona, he must have survived to continue his work in Kells and paint the Arrest and the Temptation which are incorporated in the work of Scribe C.

As for the occasion which gave rise to such an under-taking, one may remember that 797 was the second centenary of the death of St Columba, the founder of the monastery. The Book may have been begun in view of the celebration of this event and, as generally happens in such cases, it may have turned out to be a much more lengthy job than had been foreseen, so that it was not ready in time.

*Fig. 74 Ravenna, Church of S. Apollinare in Classe, marble plaque carved with peacocks and vine*

---

141. Henry, *Irish Art II*, p. 70.

*Fig. 75 Book of Kells, detail of title on f. 19v*

# APPENDIX I
## Structure of the Manuscript

This diagrammatic section of the Book of Kells is based on that made by Mr Roger Powell when he rebound the Book in 1953. Each quire (i.e. each section of vellum leaves sewn together) is numbered on the left. Folio numbers on the right (36 mistakenly occurs twice). The solid vertical lines indicate leaves which were conjoint pairs when the Book was taken to pieces in 1953. The dotted lines indicate artificial joins and stubs introduced at that rebinding. Some of these artificially joined pairs may represent original bifolia but others could never have made natural pairs. Leaves originally single often carry the most important illuminations.

| QUIRES | CONTENTS | HANDS |
|---|---|---|
| | 1  1r: Hebrew names, symbols; v: First Canon | 1r HAND A |
| **I** | 2      Table with arcades | |
| | 3  1v–5r: Canon Tables with arcades | |
| | 4 | |
| | 5 | |
| | 6  5v–6r: Canon Tables with colour bands | |
| **2** | 7  6v–7r: blank 7v: Virgin and Child | |
| | 8  8r Nativitas (Breves causae of Matthew) | |
| | 9 | |
| | 10 | |
| | 11 | |
| | 12  12r: Argumentum of Matthew | HAND A |
| | 13  13r: Breves causae of Mark | *(19 lines to the page)* |
| | 14 | |
| | 15  15v: Argumentum of Mark | |
| | 16  16v: Argumentum of Luke | |
| **3** | 17 | |
| | 18  18r: Argumentum of John | |
| | 19  19v: Breves causae of Luke | |
| | 20 | |
| | 21 | |
| | 22 | |
| | 23 | HAND B |
| | 24  24r: Breves causae of John | *(varying number of lines)* |
| | 25 | |
| ***Matthew* 4** | 26  Hebrew names | |
| | 27  27r: blank; v: four symbols | |
| | 28  28r: blank; v: portrait of Matthew | |
| | 29  29r: Liber; v: beginning of Genealogy | |
| | 30  Genealogy | 29r: *14 lines* |
| | 31     ,, | 30r–v: *12 lines* |
| | 32  32r: blank; v: portrait of Christ | 31r: *12 lines* |
| | 33  33r: Eight circles; v: blank | |
| | 34  34r: Chi-Rho | |
| **5** | 35 | |
| | 36 | |
| | 36 | |
| | 37 | |
| | 38 | |
| | 39 | |
| | 40 | |
| | 41 | |
| | 42 | |
| | 43 | |
| | 44 | |
| **6** | 45 | HAND C |
| | 46 | *(17 lines to the page)* |
| | 47 | |
| | 48 | |
| | 49 | |
| | 50 | |
| | 51 | |
| | 52 | |
| | 53 | |
| | 54 | |
| **7** | 55 | |
| | 56 | |
| | 57 | |
| | 58 | |
| | 59 | |

| QUIRES | CONTENTS | HANDS |
|---|---|---|
| | 60 | |
| | 61 | |
| | 62 | |
| | 63 | |
| **8** | 64 | |
| | 65 | |
| | 66 | |
| | 67 | |
| | 68 | |
| | 69 | |
| | 70 | |
| | 71 | |
| | 72 | |
| **9** | 73 | |
| | 74 | |
| | 75 | |
| | 76 | |
| | 77 | |
| | 78 | |
| | 79 | |
| | 80 | |
| | 81 | HAND C |
| | 82 | *(17 lines to the page)* |
| **10** | 83 | |
| | 84 | |
| | 85 | |
| | 86 | |
| | 87 | |
| | 88 | |
| | 89 | |
| | 90 | |
| | 91 | |
| | 92 | |
| **11** | 93 | |
| | 94 | |
| | 95 | |
| | 96 | |
| | 97 | |
| | 98 | |
| | 99 | |
| | 100 | |
| | 101 | |
| | 102 | |
| **12** | 103 | |
| | 104 | |
| | 105 | |
| | 106 | |
| | 107 | |
| | 108 | |
| | 109 | |
| | 110 | |
| | 111 | |
| | 112 | |
| **13** | 113 | |
| | 114  114r: Arrest; v: Tunc dicit | |
| | 115 | |
| | 116 | |
| | 117 | |

| QUIRES | | CONTENTS | HANDS | QUIRES | | CONTENTS | HANDS |
|---|---|---|---|---|---|---|---|

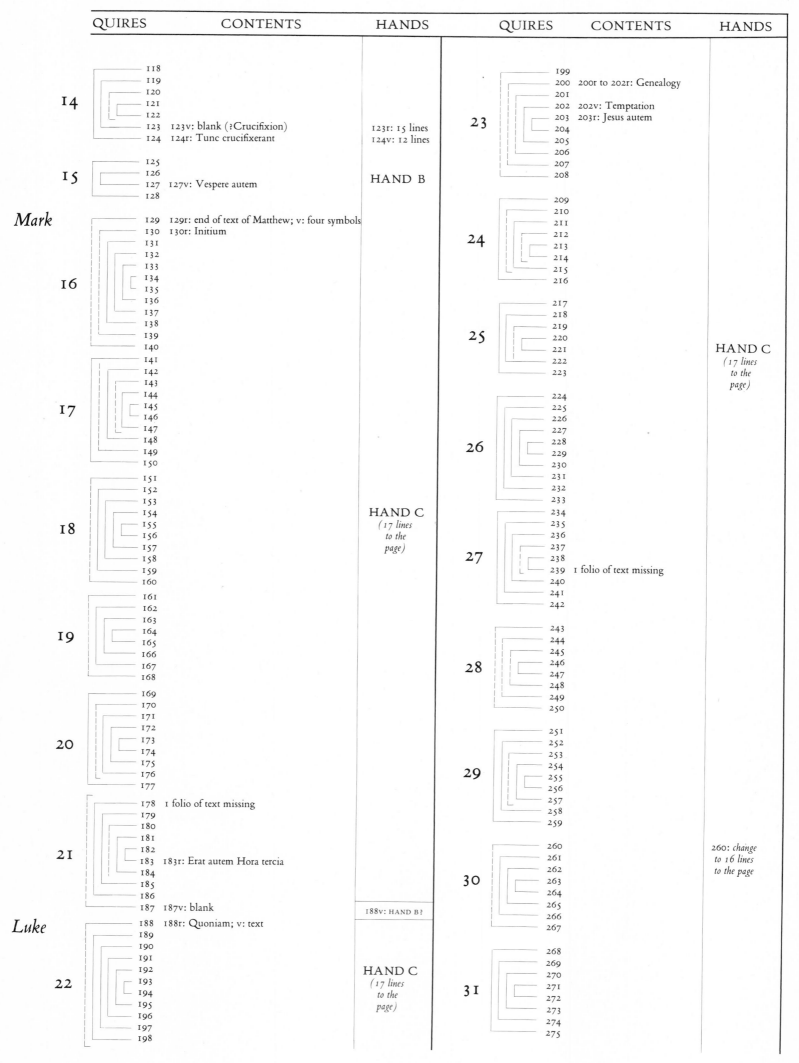

**14**
118
119
120
121
122
123    123v: blank (?Crucifixion)
124    124r: Tunc crucifixerant

123r: 15 lines
124v: 12 lines

**15**
125
126
127    127v: Vespere autem
128

HAND B

*Mark*

**16**
129    129r: end of text of Matthew; v: four symbols
130    130r: Initium
131
132
133
134
135
136
137
138
139
140

**17**
141
142
143
144
145
146
147
148
149
150

**18**
151
152
153
154
155
156
157
158
159
160

HAND C
*(17 lines to the page)*

**19**
161
162
163
164
165
166
167
168

**20**
169
170
171
172
173
174
175
176
177

**21**
178    1 folio of text missing
179
180
181
182
183    183r: Erat autem Hora tercia
184
185
186
187    187v: blank

188v: HAND B?

*Luke*

**22**
188    188r: Quoniam; v: text
189
190
191
192
193
194
195
196
197
198

HAND C
*(17 lines to the page)*

**23**
199
200    200r to 202r: Genealogy
201
202    202v: Temptation
203    203r: Jesus autem
204
205
206
207
208

**24**
209
210
211
212
213
214
215
216

**25**
217
218
219
220
221
222
223

**26**
224
225
226
227
228
229
230
231
232
233

**27**
234
235
236
237
238
239    1 folio of text missing
240
241
242

**28**
243
244
245
246
247
248
249
250

**29**
251
252
253
254
255
256
257
258
259

**30**
260
261
262
263
264
265
266
267

**31**
268
269
270
271
272
273
274
275

HAND C
*(17 lines to the page)*

260: *change to 16 lines to the page*

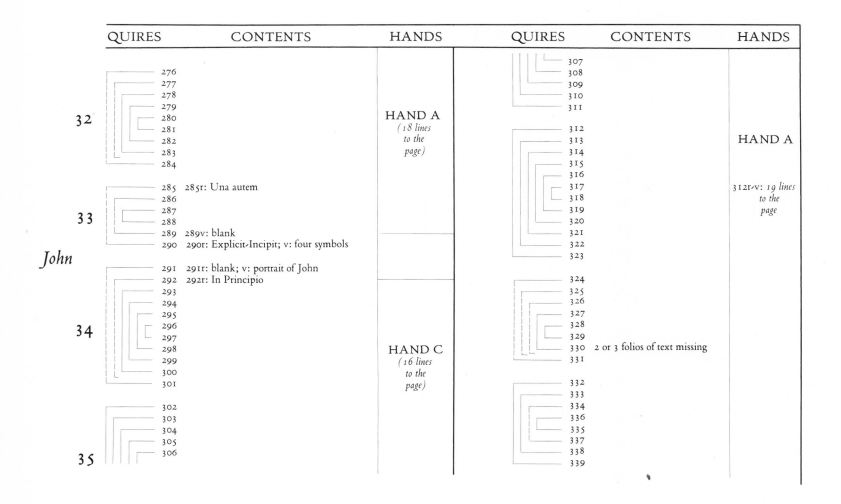

| QUIRES | CONTENTS | HANDS | QUIRES | CONTENTS | HANDS |
|---|---|---|---|---|---|

The diagram shows:

**Left side:**

Quire 32: folios 276, 277, 278, 279, 280, 281, 282, 283, 284

Quire 33: folios 285 (285r: Una autem), 286, 287, 288, 289 (289v: blank), 290 (290r: Explicit-Incipit; v: four symbols)

John

Quire 34: folios 291 (291r: blank; v: portrait of John), 292 (292r: In Principio), 293, 294, 295, 296, 297, 298, 299, 300, 301

Quire 35: folios 302, 303, 304, 305, 306

HAND A (18 lines to the page)

HAND C (16 lines to the page)

**Right side:**

folios 307, 308, 309, 310, 311

folios 312, 313, 314, 315, 316, 317, 318, 319, 320, 321, 322, 323

folios 324, 325, 326, 327, 328, 329, 330, 331 — 2 or 3 folios of text missing

folios 332, 333, 334, 336, 335, 337, 338, 339

HAND A (312r-v: 19 lines to the page)

# APPENDIX II

# List of Insular decorated manuscripts and associated manuscripts (other than the Book of Kells)

For most of these manuscripts, the essential data are found in: Kenney, *Sources*, Lowe, *C.L.A.*, Zimmermann, *Vor. Min.*, Henry, *Irish Art I* and *II* (for these abbreviations see above, p. 148).

## Ireland

MANUSCRIPTS WITH INTERNAL EVIDENCE OF ORIGIN:

The Book of Armagh (Dublin, Trinity College, MS 52), written by Ferdomnach, a scribe of Armagh in 807–8.
The Rushworth Gospels (Oxford, Bodleian Library, MS Auct.D.II.19), signed by Mac Regol, abbot of Birr, who died in 822 (he is the scribe and the painter).

MANUSCRIPTS WRITTEN BY SCRIBES WITH IRISH NAMES:

See below, Echternach.
The Grammar of Priscian in Leyden (University Library, MS Lat. 67), written by Dubtach in 838.
The Grammar of Priscian (St Gall, Cathedral Library, MS 904), written by several Irish scribes, under the direction of Maelbrigte, around 850.
The Fulda Gospels (Fulda, Library, Codex Bonifacianus III), possibly written by Cadmug, unless he was the scribe of the exemplar.

MANUSCRIPTS ASSOCIATED WITH LIBRARIES OF IRISH MONASTERIES:

The Book of Durrow (Dublin, Trinity College, MS 57), which was in the monastery of Durrow (Offaly) until the seventeenth century.
The Book of Mulling (Dublin, Trinity College, MS 60), which comes from the monastery of Tech Moling (Carlow).
The Stowe Missal and Gospel of St John (Dublin, Royal Irish Academy, MS D.II.3), which were at Lorrha (Tipperary) in the eleventh century.
The Book of Dimma (Dublin, Trinity College, MS 59), associated with Roscrea (Tipperary).

The Book of Mac Durnan (London, Lambeth Palace Library), brought to England at an early date, has from an inscription it bears an ill-defined connection with Maelbrigt Mac Durnan, abbot of Armagh from 888 to 927.

MANUSCRIPTS ASSOCIATED WITH IRISH FOUNDATIONS ON THE CONTINENT:

From the library of the monastery of *Bobbio*, in Italy, founded in the early seventh century by St Columbanus, come:
An incomplete copy of the Chronicle of Orosius (Milan, Ambrosian Library, MS D.23.sup.).

Fragments of the Commentary of St Jerome on Isaiah (palimpsest) (Milan, Ambrosian Library, MS S.45.sup.).

Fragments from a Gospel-book from Bobbio where it was already in the ninth century (Turin, University Library, MS O.IV.20). Its text had been erased, but four decorated pages subsisted; they were badly scorched in the fire of the Turin Library in 1904, but their design can still be studied.

From the library of the monastery of *St Gall* in Switzerland, founded by Gall, one of the companions of Columbanus, come the following (now in the Cathedral Library):

The Gospel-book MS 51.

The fragment of Gospel-book, MS 60.

A miscellaneous collection of written and decorated pages forming part of MS 1395.

From the Irish foundation of *Honau*, an island in the Rhine near Stras-bourg, may come MS 134 in Trier Cathedral, a Gospel-book signed in several places by Thomas, probably to be identified with an Irish abbot of that name who governed Honau from 750 to 770.

## Wales and the Border of Wales

The manuscripts which have library association with Wales and the Border of Wales are:

The Book of Lichfield, which was exchanged for a horse in the late eighth century and given to the sanctuary of S. Tellio at Llandaff where it remained until the tenth century, when it was transferred to the Cathedral of Lichfield.

A Gospel-book in the Cathedral Library at Hereford (MS P.I.2).

## Scotland

To the monastery of *Iona* can be attributed:

Perhaps the Cathach, a manuscript of the Psalms (deposited in the Royal Irish Academy), if it is accepted as having been copied by St Columba (died 597); the date is palaeographically possible. It was enshrined in Kells in the eleventh century for a member of the O'Donnell family, relatives of St Columba.

The Life of St Columba by Adamnan, copied by Dorbbéne, abbot of Iona in the first years of the eighth century, who died in 713 (Schaffhausen Library, MS 1). Decoration not very elaborate.

## England

### Lindisfarne

MANUSCRIPTS WITH INTERNAL EVIDENCE OF ORIGIN

*The Lindisfarne Gospels* (London, British Library, MS Cotton Nero D.IV) have a late, but acceptable colophon attributing them to Eadfrith, abbot of Lindisfarne from 698 to 721.

A Gospel-book in the Vatican Library (MS Barberini Lat. 570), signed by Uigbald, most probably the abbot of this name who governed Lindisfarne in the late eighth and early ninth centuries.

The Prayer-book of Cerne (Cambridge, University Library, MS L1.I.10) may, from internal evidence, come from Lindisfarne.

MANUSCRIPTS WITH LIBRARY ASSOCIATION

The library of the monastery of Lindisfarne was transferred in the ninth century to Durham, after a period spent at Chester-le-Street. The Cathedral Library in Durham contains some manuscripts of this origin:

The fragment of Gospels MS A.II.10.

The Gospel-book MS A.II.17.

A manuscript of Cassiodorus' Commentary on the Psalms (MS A.II.20).

The Gospel-book in Leningrad (State Public Library, MS Lat. F.v.I.8) may, from its analogy with the Barberini Gospel-book and the Book of Cerne, come from Lindisfarne.

### Jarrow-Wearmouth

Though the classicizing monasteries of Jarrow-Wearmouth, slightly further south than Lindisfarne, belong to a different milieu altogether, it is essential to note that the Codex Amiatinus (Florence, Laurentian Library) was copied there shortly before 716.

A copy of Bede's *Historia Ecclesiastica* (Leningrad, State Public Library, MS Lat. Q.v.I.18) can also be ascribed to the twin monasteries.

### Canterbury

Two manuscripts written in Canterbury, probably in the middle of the eighth century, also have strong connections with the Insular group:

The Codex Aureus in Stockholm (Royal Library, MS A.135).

A psalter in the British Library, London (MS Cotton Vespasian A.I).

## Manuscripts from the Anglo-Irish foundation at Echternach, in Luxembourg

The monastery of Echternach was founded in the last years of the seventh century by Willibrord, a monk from England who had spent twelve years in Ireland and may have taken some Irish monks with him when he went to the Continent. Among the books from the monastery's library now in the Bibliothèque Nationale in Paris are:

The Echternach Gospels (MS Lat. 9389).

The Book of the Prophets (MS Lat. 9382), signed by Vergilius, the usual Latin equivalent of the Irish name Ferghil or Fergus.

A Martyrologium signed by Laurentius and a Calendar bound with it.

In addition:

The Maihingen Gospels (now at Schloss Harburg, Coll. Oettingen-Wallerstein) may also come from the library of Echternach. From an acrostic it contains the book seems to be due to a pupil of Laurentius.

MANUSCRIPTS WITHOUT ORIGIN OR LIBRARY ASSOCIATION

A certain number of manuscripts have no indication of either scribe, date or library. The chief ones are:

A Gospel-book now divided between the library of Corpus Christi College in Cambridge (MS 197) and the British Library in London (MS Cotton Otho C.V).

An incomplete Gospel-book in the Bodleian Library, Oxford (MS Rawlinson G.167).

The *Collectio Canonum* in Cologne Cathedral (MS 213).

A Gospel-book and fragments kept in the Church of St Catherine in Maeseyck (Belgium), thought at one time to have been written in the monastery of Alden Eyck.

# INDEX

Numbers in brackets refer to notes by page
Numbers in italics refer to figures by figure numbers

PHOTOGRAPHIC ACKNOWLEDGMENTS

The black and white photographs are mostly from the Archives of the Department of Archaeology, University College, Dublin. For supplying them or for permission to take them we are glad to thank the authorities of the Libraries quoted in the captions. We are also grateful to Mrs. G.L. Marsh-Micheli for figures 11, 26a and 46a, to Belzeaux-Zodiaque for figures 5, 21, 26b, 40, 45 and 61b, and to Mr. Liam de Paor for figure 37.